GO CRUISING!

A young crew's guide to
sailing and motor cruisers

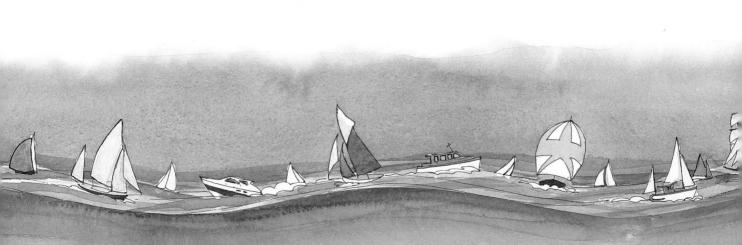

CONTENTS

Foreword by Tom Cunliffe

Watching my own child grow up as part of the team aboard my family cruising yacht has been one of the greatest delights of my life. Society is increasingly lacking in direct physical realities, and the adventures we have shared on the water have given us a sense of mutual history that holds us together in a way little else could.

Reading has always been a vital part of my daughter's on-board experience, from Where the Wild Things Are, she progressed through Swallows and Amazons to Hornblower and Conrad, but nothing was produced specifically for kids like her, acquiring the skills of living on board and becoming a useful crew. I've thoroughly enjoyed dipping into Claudia Myatt's earlier illustrated books, but it's in Go Cruising! that she has really hit the spot for children like mine. The pictures are as friendly as ever, and the tiny figures asking those insistent questions tickle me to death, but what I admire most is the way she has tackled serious subjects such as Navigation and Rules of the Road. Capturing the interest of youthful minds in these areas is an achievement to be proud of. The result will be a generation of youngsters who can't wait to

clamber on board. Their parents will have more fun, and families who are happy together at sea grow closer as the years pass.

Come to think of it, this is more than a children's book. For all its clever disguise, the technical content is so good I might just recommend it to some of my Yachtmaster candidates....

Tom Cunliffe – RYA Yachtmaster Examiner

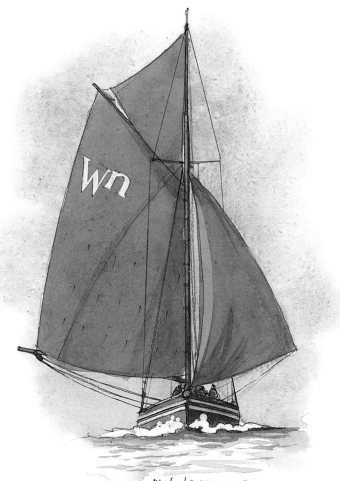

"Westernman"

WHAT IS CRUISING?

Cruising is about travelling by boat, just for the fun of it. It involves sleeping on board, eating on board and living afloat.

Cruising can be for a weekend, a week, or a lifetime. You can cruise up a creek, down the coast or round the world - but it all starts with a boat....

To go cruising you need a boat big enough to sleep on. It might be a sailing or a motor boat, belonging to family, friends, or a hire company. Let's start by learning a few boaty words....

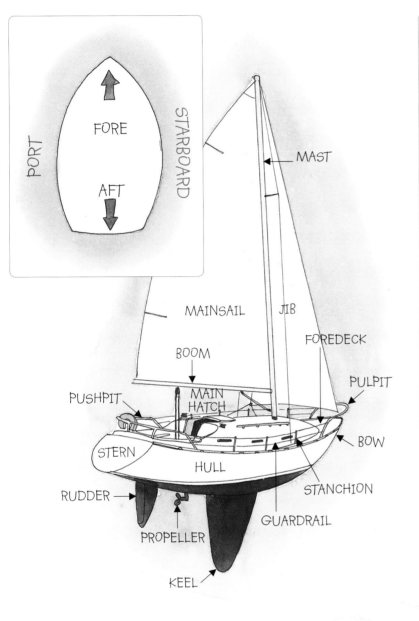

WHO'S WHO ON BOARD?

The SKIPPER is the boss – whether it's your mum, dad, friend or total stranger they're in charge of the boat.

...not unless you say 'please'!

The HELMSMAN is whoever is steering the boat at the time. 'Take the helm' means it's your turn to steer.

CREW – that's you! Learn as much as you can about how the boat works if you want to be an able seaman rather than an unable seaman!

Incompetent crew   Competent crew

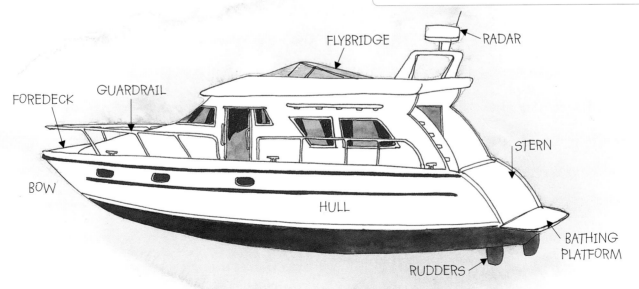

Big boats, small boats, sail boats, motor boats - cruisers come in all shapes and sizes. Here are a few sailing yachts to start off with....

At just over 6 metres, cruisers don't get much smaller than this two berth modern classic.

A modern family cruiser like this can range from 7 metres up to about 20 metres.

This ocean going ketch (two masted) can take you anywhere you want to go.

A motor sailer combines a big engine with a set of sails – and has a wheelhouse to keep you dry while steering!

A catamaran has two hulls which gives it a wide and spacious cabin.

There are three basic types of motor cruiser, based on their hull shape and engine size. They usually have two powerful diesel engines, though others may only have one.

VERY FAST

A planing boat has powerful engines and is shaped to skim over the water – very fast but a bumpy ride in rough weather!

A semi-displacement cruiser is a mix of the two types – its bow rises out of the water at high speeds.

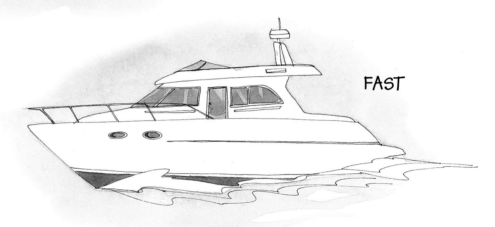

FAST

NOT SO FAST!

A displacement cruiser is a little ship – heavy and stable it pushes its way through the water. Good for long trips as it's very seaworthy.

OIL PRINCESS

Can you spare a bit of diesel...

How far can a cruiser go? A seaworthy motor cruiser can cross an ocean but it is limited by the amount of fuel it can carry.

Small sailing boats can cross big oceans as long as they can cope with bad weather. The main limitation is how much food, water and gear they can carry.

Let's have a look below decks. There are some more new words to learn as you go down the COMPANIONWAY (the steps into the cabin) into the SALOON (the main living space).

How do you spell 'MUTINY'?

Cupboards will all have secure catches to stop them flying open at sea. Find out how they work before trying to pull them open!

The CHART TABLE and navigation instruments will be near the companionway. Don't leave clutter here or you'll have a cross navigator.

The little cabin at the front is called the FORECABIN or FOC'SLE (pronounced folk-sul). It usually has two berths. The toilet on a boat is called the HEAD.

The saloon table has a rim around it called a FIDDLE RAIL, to stop things sliding off. The table may also drop down to make a double berth.

The kitchen is called the GALLEY.

The cooker may be on GIMBALS, which means it can stay level when the boat isn't! It will also have a rail around the burners to hold pans in place.

SAILING CRUISER

MOTOR CRUISER

A motor cruiser will probably have its steering position in the main saloon.

The galley will be more like your kitchen at home, with a built-in cooker rather than gimballed.

Motor cruisers have bigger, wider cabins than sailing cruisers, with bigger windows. Like sailing cruisers there will be fiddle rails round tables and shelves, and the cupboards will have safety catches.

All cruisers have limited storage space – you'll have to learn to be tidy!

What do you take with you when you go cruising? In a cool climate you'll need layers of warm clothes, a fleecy top, warm hat and some decent waterproofs. In a hot climate take warmer clothes for evening and clothes that protect you from the sun.

Be prepared for all kinds of weather - if it's hot you'll need sunhat, shades and lashings of sun cream.

Remember the effects of the sun are always more intense at sea.

On your feet.... You'll need wellies and deck shoes (sandals or trainers are fine as long as they have non marking soles).

Even on a large boat storage space is limited and cupboards are always odd shaped. Use soft bags that squidge into small spaces.

BAD IDEA

GOOD IDEA

What else can you take?

On your own boat you can leave lots of things on board, but on someone else's boat you'll have to be clever about what you take. Playing cards, books, sketch pad, music with headphones, camera, can all be squeezed into a small bag.

Stay safe – before going any closer to the water, let's look at lifejackets. You'll need one that fits properly – an adult lifejacket won't work on a child. Get used to wearing your lifejacket all the time you're on or near the water. There are two basic types:

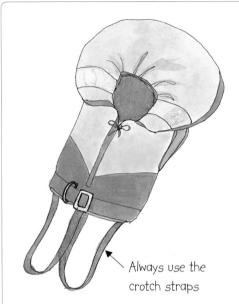

Always use the crotch straps

This full buoyancy child's lifejacket will keep you fully supported with your head clear of the water.

Disadvantage: the bulky collar takes a bit of getting used to and can be uncomfortable in hot weather.

Advantage: wear this type when you're playing in or around the water and you'll get to know how well it works!

This automatic lifejacket stays flat until you hit the water and then whoosh – a small gas cylinder inflates it to full buoyancy.

Advantage: very lightweight and comfortable to wear.

Disadvantage: once it's inflated you need to repack it with a new gas cylinder again. If you fall overboard your parents will *be* more than happy to pay for a new cylinder, but if it inflates by accident while messing around in the dinghy, you may have to dig into your pocket money!

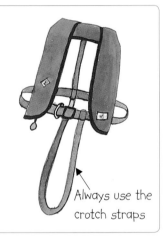

Always use the crotch straps

This is a buoyancy aid NOT a lifejacket - it can only help a swimmer to stay afloat and is generally used by dinghy sailors.

If you can swim, it's a good idea to use one if you're playing close to shore or in the dinghy and don't want to set off your automatic lifejacket!

Not unless I can wear my lifejacket and lifeline!

Last but not least....

Clip one end to your lifejacket harness....

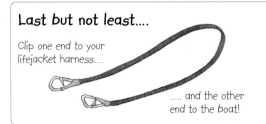

..... and the other end to the boat!

This is a lifeline which helps keep you attached to the boat – use it in rough weather, at night, or whenever the skipper says so!

WELCOME ABOARD!

CREW JOB LIST

- Avoid falling in the water

- Move around the deck without tripping over

- Don't treat the cabin like a house

- Cast off mooring lines and coil them up

- Put fenders away without dropping them in the water

Marinas are like car parks for boats, so you just stroll down and step on board, don't you? Well yes, but you have to think like a sailor the minute you step onto the pontoon. Start by putting your lifejacket on before you go through the gate!

Be careful not to trip over any loose mooring lines or cleats (the metal things the ropes are tied onto).

Don't run! Marinas can be wobbly, especially finger pontoons - the little ones inbetween the boats.

Marinas float! On tidal coasts, they go up and down with the tide so the bridge can be very steep at low tide. If there's no tide, or if the marina is inside lock gates, you can step straight onto the pontoon.

WATCH OUT! Anchors over the bow can overhang the pontoon at head height.

WATCH OUT! Playing with the marina trolleys is a really bad idea. Don't even think about it.

Dad says if you're not out in five minutes we'll miss the tide

Marinas have showers and toilets - use these and not the ones on board when you're here.

Marinas are fun places too - great for crabbing!

It's time to learn some more boat words, this time so you can find out how to move around safely, what you can hold onto and what you need to avoid tripping over.

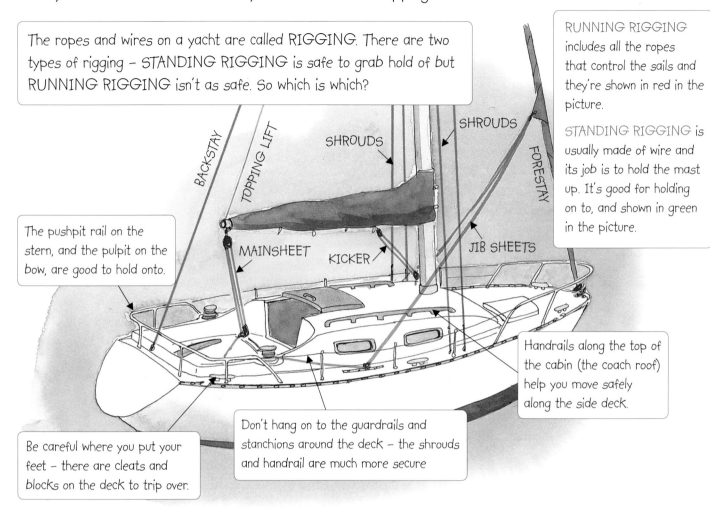

The ropes and wires on a yacht are called RIGGING. There are two types of rigging – STANDING RIGGING is safe to grab hold of but RUNNING RIGGING isn't as safe. So which is which?

RUNNING RIGGING includes all the ropes that control the sails and they're shown in red in the picture.

STANDING RIGGING is usually made of wire and its job is to hold the mast up. It's good for holding on to, and shown in green in the picture.

The pushpit rail on the stern, and the pulpit on the bow, are good to hold onto.

BACKSTAY
TOPPING LIFT
SHROUDS
SHROUDS
FORESTAY
MAINSHEET
KICKER
JIB SHEETS

Handrails along the top of the cabin (the coach roof) help you move safely along the side deck.

Be careful where you put your feet – there are cleats and blocks on the deck to trip over.

Don't hang on to the guardrails and stanchions around the deck – the shrouds and handrail are much more secure

The deck layout of a motor cruiser is a lot simpler than a sailing boat – but it's tricky to move around when you're travelling at speed!

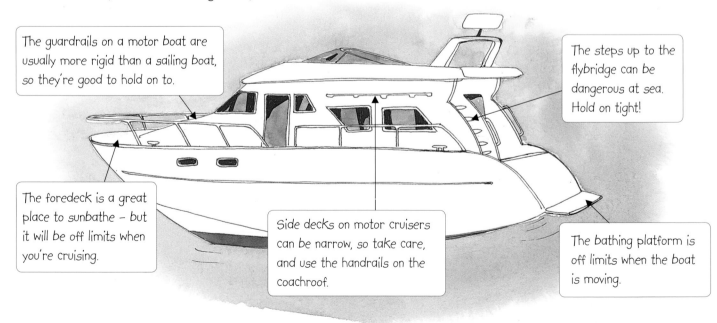

The guardrails on a motor boat are usually more rigid than a sailing boat, so they're good to hold on to.

The steps up to the flybridge can be dangerous at sea. Hold on tight!

The foredeck is a great place to sunbathe – but it will be off limits when you're cruising.

Side decks on motor cruisers can be narrow, so take care, and use the handrails on the coachroof.

The bathing platform is off limits when the boat is moving.

How do you step on board? Sometimes it's easy, sometimes it's not so easy. Big boats may have steps alongside, but on a small sailing boat you have to climb over the side like this....

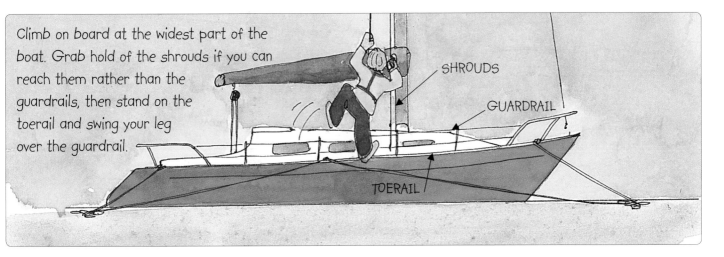

Climb on board at the widest part of the boat. Grab hold of the shrouds if you can reach them rather than the guardrails, then stand on the toerail and swing your leg over the guardrail.

SHROUDS

GUARDRAIL

TOERAIL

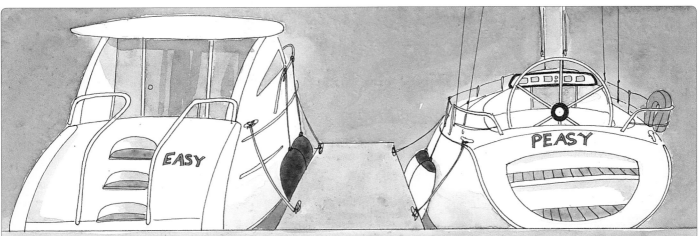

EASY

PEASY

Sometimes you have to get on board over the stern – this is very common in the Mediterranean. Many modern boats have steps cut into the stern to make it easy.

If a boat is kept on a mooring, you'll get taken out in a dinghy. Climbing onto a big boat from a wobbly small boat can be tricky – go slowly and carefully.

Kneel on the toe rail if you can't reach to stand on it.

SHROUDS

HANDRAIL

Bring your fingers in before the dinghy comes alongside or they'll get squashed!

Step from the middle of the dinghy (not the side) onto the toe rail, holding onto the shrouds if you can reach them, then swing your leg over the guardrail.

BELOW DECKS... The cabin of a modern cruiser is very comfortable with many of the things you have at home.

But never forget you're in something that's moving all the time. You need to think like a sailor below decks as well as on deck.

Tidy stowage is important!

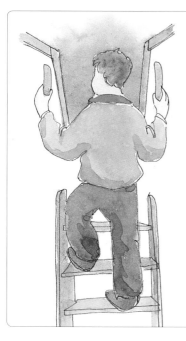

Cabins are full of useful handholds – find out where they all are, especially the ones you can reach!

A sailing boat may have steep steps down the companionway into the cabin, so use the handholds and go downstairs backwards.

Always switch off lights, cd player and anything else that uses electricity as soon as you've finished with it. Electricity on board comes from the boat's batteries which need charging from the engine, so don't waste it, especially on a sailing boat.

I'm conserving energy....

Water is precious on board – a boat will only carry what can fit in its tanks. The tap may look the same as the one at home but don't leave it running while you clean your teeth. There may be a salt water tap as well as fresh water tap, so find out which is which!

Also check if the tap water is drinkable.

Which one is ginger beer?

Learn how to use the toilet before you need to go! It's more complicated than flushing at home, so get someone to show you how.

Don't use the toilet in harbour, and avoid putting anything down it that could block the pipes.

'Open valve A, pump handle ten times, close valve A, open valve B, pump handle....'

SAFETY CHECK! If it's your first time aboard, the skipper will give you a safety briefing and tell you the rules of the boat. You'll be told all about the safety gear the boat carries, where it's kept and how it's used. Here are a few basic safety items; see how many you can find when you get on board.

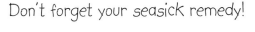
Don't forget your seasick remedy!

If you think you might be queasy out at sea, the time to take something is while you're still in harbour. More on coping with seasickness in Chapter Five.

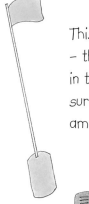

This is a danbuoy – thrown to someone in the water it makes sure they can be seen amongst the waves.

A lifebuoy and light, to be thrown to a man overboard to help them float and be seen.

Fire extinguishers will be in the cabin close to the galley and engine compartment.

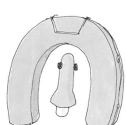

A vhf/dsc radio is used for communicating with other boats and with the coastguard. It is also to call for help in an emergency.

Emergency flares will be kept in a locker close to the deck; these are set off to attract attention in an emergency.

The most important safety rule of all is DON'T FALL OVERBOARD! Even on a calm day a sudden movement or wash from another boat can make you lose your balance.

A boat travelling offshore will have a liferaft. If the boat sinks it can be automatically inflated to keep everyone safe.

Think like a sailor – always hold on to something secure!

The one I caught yesterday was as big as.....

..... this!

CASTING OFF! Mooring lines (also called warps) tie the boat to the pontoon with cleats like this:

Find out where these are on deck so that –
a) you can use them when asked and
b) you don't trip over them!

To cast off a mooring line, the line needs to be untied on the pontoon, looped around the cleat and then brought back on board, like this. This is called putting the lines on a slip.

Don't let the rope go slack while you're holding onto it. It helps to hold it tight if you hook the end you're holding round the corner of the cleat while you're waiting to let go.

HOW TO SECURE A ROPE ON A CLEAT - although you'll be untying a cleat before you have to tie one, let's look at how it's done so that you can have a bit of practice.

1. Take a turn around the base of the cleat

2. Make a figure of eight over the ends

3. Make another figure of eight if you can

4. Finish off by taking another turn round the base of the cleat

When given the order 'let go forward' (or 'let go aft' if you're at the back of the boat) drop the rope then pull in the slack as quick as you can.

All clear!

The rope should run freely round the cleat so you can pull it in quickly. Once it's all in, you can untie the end attached to the boat.

Let the skipper know when the line is clear of the pontoon.

As you bring the mooring lines in, don't let them trail over the side in case they get caught round the propeller.

All clear!

When in harbour, fenders are tied to the boat to protect the hull. As soon as you leave, it will be the crew's job to bring the fenders in.

Before you put them away, have a go at tying them on so you can learn how it's done. The most common way is with a knot called a ROUND TURN AND TWO HALF HITCHES.

Bring the fenders onto the deck before you take them off, then they won't fall into the sea if you lose your grip while untying them!

BUTTERFINGERS

HOW TO TIE ON A FENDER WITH A ROUND TURN AND TWO HALF HITCHES

Loop the free end of the rope twice around the rail.

Make a half hitch round the standing (fixed) part of the rope.

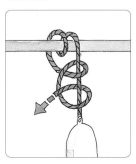

Then make another half hitch and pull tight.

If you leave a loop in the last hitch, like you do with shoelaces, it will be quick to undo.

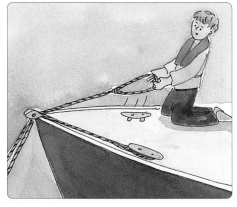

LEAVING A MOORING is simpler than leaving a pontoon as there are fewer ropes to deal with. A mooring buoy is tied on with one or sometimes two ropes which just need to be untied and dropped in the water. Often the mooring line has a loop on the end which is just hooked over the cleat.

Don't let go of the mooring line until the skipper has given the word.

When the line is free, call out 'All clear'.

Once all the mooring lines are on board it's the crew's job to coil them up and put them away. If you get a chance to practise this before you sail, you'll impress your skipper!

Step One

If you're right handed, make the coils with your right hand and hold them with your left. If you're left handed do it the other way round.

Step Two

The secret of a good coil is to twist your right hand outwards as you make each coil. This stops the rope kinking up. If you're not sure, get someone to show you.

Step Three

To keep the coils the same length, use the width of your arms each time.

Oops!

How not to coil a rope.... If your coil ends up looking like this, then you haven't been twisting your wrist with each coil. Go back to step two and have another go.

When you get to the end, check with your skipper how he likes his coils finished off. The way shown here is useful if your coil is to be hung on a hook. When you've coiled the line, pick up one of the loops, bring it round the coils (several times if necessary), through the middle and over the top like this. If the rope is being hung on a hook, stop at stage three and hang it with the loop you've just pulled through. If it's going in a locker, you can finish it off by pulling the final loop over the top of the coil (step 4).

SET SAIL!

CREW JOB LIST

- Help to hoist and trim the sails

- Use winches without mangling fingers

- Know what to do when tacking and gybing

- Avoid falling overboard

Now we're finally heading out to sea! This chapter is for all on sailing boats, to help you get to grips with all those sails and ropes, but don't skip it if you're cruising a motor boat - it's useful to know how sailing boats work when it comes to avoiding collisions.

Most yachts set two sails, MAINSAIL and JIB. Ropes that pull sails up are called HALYARDS and ropes that control the sails are called SHEETS. There are other sails and other ropes, but if you can remember these it's a good start!

You'll probably leave the marina under engine and get sail up in clear water, but the sails will be made ready for hoisting before you leave. If you're leaving from a mooring buoy, you may be setting off under sail if conditions are right.

Let's start with hoisting the MAINSAIL....

Pull the halyard down to hoist the sail up. You don't need big muscles - lean your weight back on the rope with the free end round a cleat, and then take up the slack.

This is called 'sweating up' the halyard.

The sail cover can be taken off before you leave harbour. The sail ties come off just before you hoist.

The topping lift holds the boom up - slacken this off once the sail is up.

KICKER

MAINSHEET

The mainsheet controls the mainsail and the kicker holds the boom down. These both need to be loose while you hoist.

HOW TO COIL A HALYARD AND HANG IT ON A CLEAT

When you've made the coil, put your hand through and hold the last uncoiled bit....

.... pull this through the coil and twist it so you have a loop.

.... take this loop and hook it over the top of the cleat. Neat.

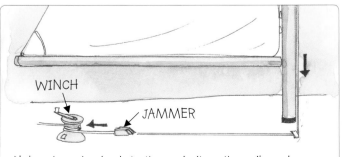

WINCH

JAMMER

Halyard running back to the cockpit so the sail can be hoisted from there.

On many boats the halyard will run across the coachroof back to the cockpit, so that the sail can be hoisted from the cockpit.

There will be a winch to help take the strain and a jammer to fix the halyard in place - more about winches and jammers later in this chapter.

HOISTING THE JIB - There are two common types of jib; most modern yachts have a roller furling jib which is really easy as it's rolled round the forestay. This is quite big when unrolled and sometimes called a genoa or jenny. A conventional jib has to be clipped onto the forestay and hoisted with a halyard.

Jibs have two sheets, one each side of the mast. Only the downwind (leeward) sheet is used, and the sheet not in use is called the lazy sheet.

ROLLER FURLING JIB

Releasing the furling line and pulling on the leeward (downwind) sheet unwinds the sail - easy!

All the corners and sides of a sail have names too, so if you're good at learning boat words, have a go at these.

MORE SAILOR-SPEAK

I'm going as fast as I can!

Make that fast!

If you're asked to make a rope fast, it just means secure it to a cleat or jammer so that it doesn't move.

A conventional jib is fastened to the forestay with clips called hanks. The halyard is attached to the top and up it goes. A boat will have different size jibs to use with different wind strengths.

When taking the sail out of its bag, always tie the bag onto something so it doesn't blow away.

HOW ROPES ARE HELD IN PLACE. In a dinghy you can hold onto sheets when controlling sails, but in a yacht the forces involved are much stronger, so cleats, jammers and winches are used to take the strain. It's important to know how to use these safely so that you end up with the same number of fingers you started with!

WINCHES

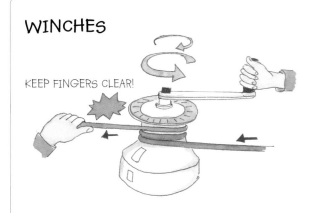

KEEP FINGERS CLEAR!

Winches help you to pull in ropes when they get too tough to pull by hand.

Always take the rope CLOCKWISE round the winch. Make at least two turns and get someone to hold the free end tight while you turn the handle. Some winches have two gears, so if one way gets too hard to turn, try the other. When you've got your rope tight enough, cleat it off (don't let it slip!), take the winch handle out and put it away.

Some winches are self tailing which means there's a groove at the top to keep the rope tight for you.

This also holds the rope in place when you've finished winching so you don't need to cleat it off.

How do you let a rope out again? Very carefully! To let a little bit out, when trimming a sheet, put the flat of your hand against the winch like this, keep tension on the line and ease out gently. If you want to get the rope off a winch quickly, when the pressure has come off the rope, flick it upwards like this so it can run out freely.

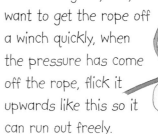

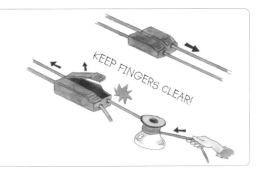

JAMMERS
Sometimes ropes are held in place by jammers like this. When closed, you can pull the rope in and the jammer will stop it slipping back again.

To let the rope out, you have to lift the handle - but to save losing your fingers, take a few turns around the winch first to take the strain before opening the jammer so you can ease it out gently.

KEEP FINGERS CLEAR!

DON'T DO IT!
Never wrap a rope around your hand.

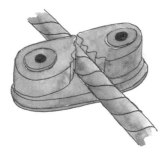

This is a CAM CLEAT - you'll probably find one of these on the mainsheet.

It grips the rope tightly and lets you pull it in without slipping back. Then when you need to release it quickly you just pull it upwards out of the cleat.

WIND POWER! A yacht can sail in any direction except directly into the wind. About 40 degrees off the wind is about as close as you can get in a modern yacht. A good sailor is always wind-aware, so get into the habit of working out where the wind is coming from and how hard it is blowing.

These are the POINTS OF SAILING with some new words to learn.

As the boat changes direction, the sails need pulling in (sheeting in) or letting out (easing). This is called TRIMMING the sails.

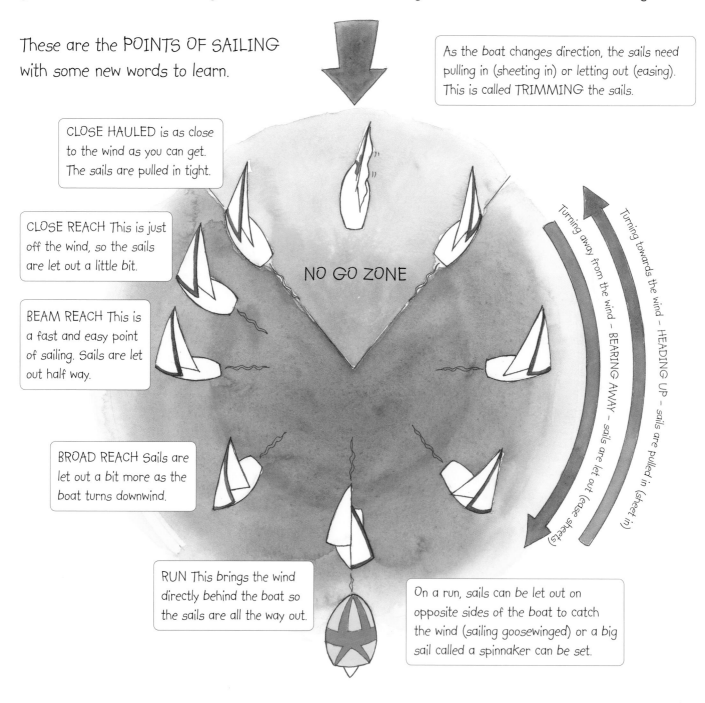

CLOSE HAULED is as close to the wind as you can get. The sails are pulled in tight.

CLOSE REACH This is just off the wind, so the sails are let out a little bit.

BEAM REACH This is a fast and easy point of sailing. Sails are let out half way.

BROAD REACH Sails are let out a bit more as the boat turns downwind.

RUN This brings the wind directly behind the boat so the sails are all the way out.

NO GO ZONE

Turning away from the wind – BEARING AWAY – sails are let out (ease sheets)

Turning towards the wind – HEADING UP – sails are pulled in (sheet in)

On a run, sails can be let out on opposite sides of the boat to catch the wind (sailing goosewinged) or a big sail called a spinnaker can be set.

WINDWARD AND LEEWARD

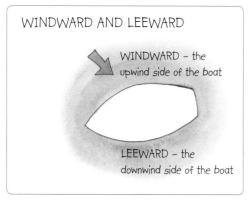

WINDWARD – the upwind side of the boat

LEEWARD – the downwind side of the boat

WHICH TACK AM I ON?

When the wind is blowing over the port side of the boat, you're on PORT TACK. When the wind is blowing over the starboard side of the boat, you're on STARBOARD TACK. If you're sailing downwind, look at which side the mainsail is out (mainsail on port side means you're on starboard tack).

HOW DO SAILS WORK? As you can *see*, there's more to sailing than *being blown along*! Boats can sail upwind because the way the wind flows past the sails works in a similar way to an aeroplane wing where the difference in pressure gives 'lift'.

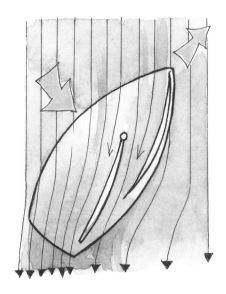

The resistance of the *keel* below the water converts this sideways pressure into forward motion. Without a *keel* the yacht would go sideways as much as forwards (this is called 'making leeway' and all boats do it a bit.)

When sailing close hauled, the sideways pressure on the sails is at its strongest and the boat will heel over. This can be quite alarming until you get used to it but don't worry - the weight of the keel underneath the water will act against that pressure to stop the boat going over too far. This is how it works....

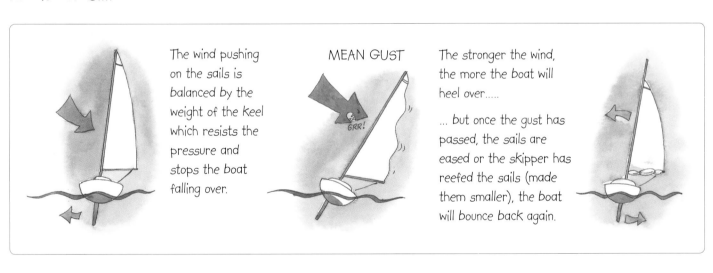

The wind pushing on the sails is balanced by the weight of the keel which resists the pressure and stops the boat falling over.

MEAN GUST

GRR!

The stronger the wind, the more the boat will heel over.....

... but once the gust has passed, the sails are eased or the skipper has reefed the sails (made them smaller), the boat will bounce back again.

DON'T PANIC! A yacht is quite happy sailing at a slight angle. If she goes too far the skipper will do something about it, but whatever happens you won't capsize!

EVEN KEEL

SAILING UPWIND You can't sail directly into the wind, so if that's the direction you want to go you have to sail a zig zag course from close hauled to close hauled either side of the no go zone. This is called BEATING TO WINDWARD and involves turning the bow of the boat through the wind so that the sails change sides (TACKING). This is how it goes....

1. Make sure the windward sheet is ready to pull in, then watch the jib.

2. The helmsman will call out 'lee-oh' as he starts the turn. Don't let the jib sheet go yet - watch the jib and wait until the boat is in the eye of the wind.

3. Let off the jib sheet (mind your fingers!) when the bow passes through the eye of the wind.

4. Pull in the slack on the new sheet as quickly as you can before the wind fills the sail.

5. When it gets too hard to pull by hand, use the winch handle for the last bit of pull. If it's not a self tailing winch, get someone to hold the end tight for you.

How do you know how far to sheet in? See if the jib has telltales like these.

Leeward (outside) telltale flapping means it's sheeted in too far.

Windward (inside) telltale flapping means it's not sheeted in far enough.

Both in line - perfect!

SAILING DOWNWIND When sailing downwind the sails are out as far as they can go to catch as much wind as possible and let it blow you along. Having the wind behind you may feel relaxing, but it's not all plain sailing....

When sailing downwind, you may not be allowed to sit on the coachroof....

WATCH OUT FOR....

.... because if the boat wobbles, the boom can flip across accidentally – with force! This is called an accidental GYBE.

.... A GYBE!!

CLONK!

DOWNWIND TRICKS....

If the wind is exactly astern you can sail goosewinged - with jib and main out either side. A pole can be used to hold the jib out, and sometimes a preventer is rigged - a rope leading forward from the end of the boom to stop the boom coming across accidentally.

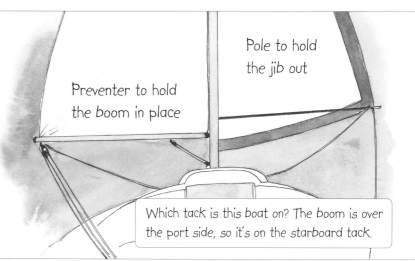

Pole to hold the jib out

Preventer to hold the boom in place

Which tack is this boat on? The boom is over the port side, so it's on the starboard tack.

SPINNAKER

- a big balloon shaped sail made of light material, designed to catch as much wind as possible. It has lots of control lines so it usually needs several crew members to set and trim.

CRUISING CHUTE

- made of similar material but simpler to rig - like a big genoa. It's not so good when the wind is directly astern but great on a broad reach.

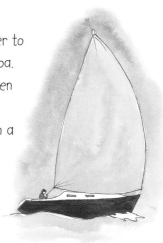

Changing direction downwind can mean bringing the sails to the other side of the boat, just like tacking. The difference between tacking and gybing is that when you gybe you bring the stern of the boat through the wind; when you tack you bring the bow of the boat through the wind. This is how gybing goes....

The most important thing during a gybe is not to let the boom come across too quickly – it has a long way to go and can be dangerous if it's not controlled!

STAND BY TO GYBE!

READY!

GYBE-OH!

WIND

Broad reaching on the starboard tack

Wind astern

Broad reaching on the port tack

Jib sheets are made ready and mainsail is sheeted in.

The helmsman begins the turn. As the boom flips over, the crew change the headsail sheets and the mainsheet is eased out.

The helmsman settles the boat on the new course with the wind on the quarter while the crew make adjustments to sail trim.

The crew's job when gybing is very similar to tacking - changing the jib sheets from one side the other - but because the jib is not pulled in tight, it's possible to tie off the windward sheet before letting go the leeward sheet. Then you can trim it once the boat is on its new course, so you don't have all that heavy winching in to do when you gybe!

Crew can tie off the new jib sheet before letting go of the other one....

The helmsman or a crew member will sheet the mainsail in before the boat turns.

Once the sails have changed sides, the old sheet can be let off and the new one trimmed.

The mainsail can also be eased right out.

TAKE THE HELM!

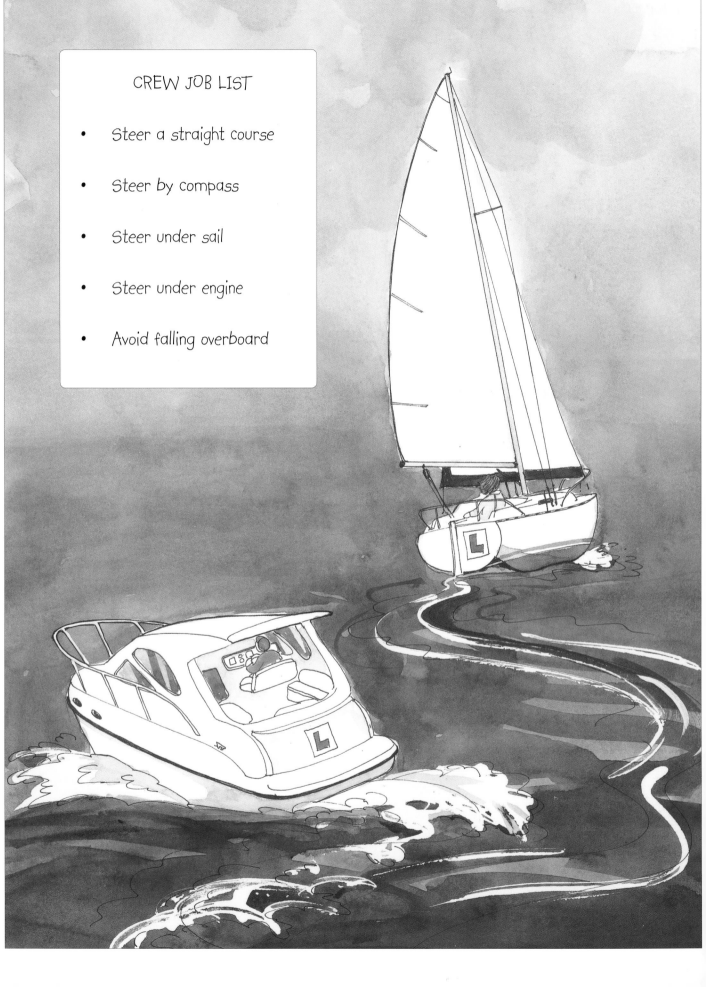

CREW JOB LIST

- Steer a straight course

- Steer by compass

- Steer under sail

- Steer under engine

- Avoid falling overboard

STEERING - Boats are steered with a tiller or a wheel which work by turning the boat's rudder. The tiller is directly connected to the rudder, the wheel is connected through a series of gears and links. Let's look first at how tiller steering works....

Sit wherever you can *see* best. This is usually the upwind side.

A yacht will pivot around its keel.

Push the tiller in the opposite direction to the way you want to turn. Remember a yacht will *be* slower to respond than a dinghy.

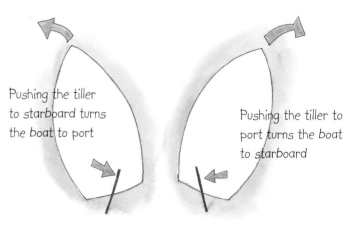

Pushing the tiller to starboard turns the boat to port

Pushing the tiller to port turns the boat to starboard

Some yachts, and all motor boats, have wheel steering. In some ways this is easier, as you turn the wheel the way you want to go, like a car. It can be tricky knowing how far you've turned the rudder when you turn the wheel or how to bring the rudder back to the middle. Have a look at the wheel - there will normally *be* something on it to show the centre position.

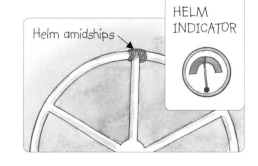

Helm amidships

HELM INDICATOR

Looks like Harry's got new crew again.....

The tiller or wheel is called the HELM, and the person steering is called the HELMSMAN (even when she's a girl!)

You only need small adjustments of the helm to steer a straight course!. If you get in a muddle, bring the tiller or wheel back to the middle, let the boat settle, and try again.

HOW DO YOU KNOW WHICH WAY TO STEER? When you're close to shore and there are things to see, choose a fixed object as your reference point to steer for, like a buoy or landmark. There may also be tides to take into account, but more about those later....

DIRECTION IN RELATION TO THE BOAT - these terms are useful to know so you can understand what's meant when told to keep the wind on your port quarter and aim for a buoy on the starboard bow!

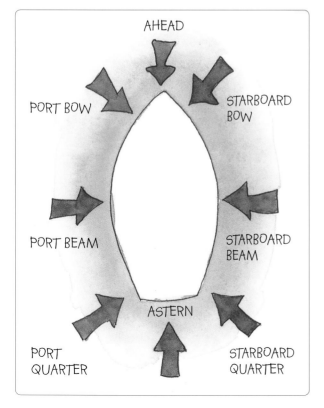

A good helmsman also needs to learn how to steer a COMPASS COURSE. This takes practice, especially working out which way to turn the helm when you go off course!

The first thing to learn is what all those numbers on the steering compass mean....

The compass shows MAGNETIC north which is a few degrees different from TRUE north

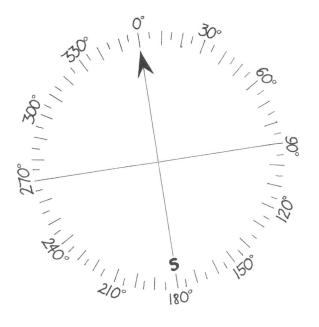

A BIT OF MATHEMATICS....
(but not too much!)

Instead of north, south, east and west, a steering compass is divided into 360 degrees, just like a circle. So, north is 0 degrees, east is 90, south is 180 and west is 270.

It helps to remember that the numbers go clockwise round the circle - so if you're steering 40 degrees but should be steering 60 degrees, then you'll know that turning to starboard will bring you to higher numbers.

Imagine you've been asked to steer 60 degrees. When you're at the helm, the steering compass looks like this....

Don't keep your eyes glued to the compass! Just glance at it frequently to check you're on course.

When it all gets too confusing, it helps to remember that the compass is the only thing on board that stays still. It's the boat that's turning! (Even more confused....??)

Oops, off course to starboard. Push the tiller to starboard or turn the wheel to port.

Spot on!

Oops, off course to port.
Push the tiller to port or turn the wheel to starboard.

STEERING UNDER SAIL means you have to be constantly aware of the direction of the wind in relation to the boat. There are lots of clues to help you - the feel of the wind on your face, a wind vane at the top of the mast, the pattern of the waves, electronic wind instruments - use them all!

STEERING UPWIND can be tricky, especially when you're close hauled which is as close to the wind as you can go. This means that the slightest wobble from the helmsman can put the bow too close to the wind and take you into the no-go zone.

Turning into the wind is called LUFFING, as it makes the luff of the sail flap. You know when it's happened because the boat will stop.

Don't let this put you off, have a go - you'll soon get the feel of it.

Sometimes you luff on purpose, if you want to stop the boat.

This is how the wind indicator on the top of the mast works. (This is a seagull's eye view, but you should be able to see it clearly from the cockpit). The arrow on the windvane points into the wind - so if the tail of the arrow goes into the V shaped bit then you're in the no go zone!

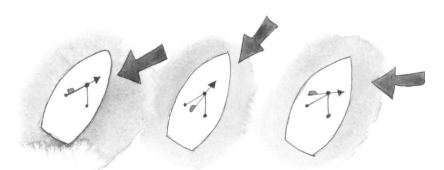

This is an electronic wind indicator - the needle shows you where the wind is coming from. This boat is close hauled on the starboard tack.

Close hauled on the starboard tack - the tail of the arrow is on the edge of the no go zone.

When the tail of the arrow is in the no go zone the boat is head to wind and the boat will stop.

Close reaching on the starboard tack with the wind just off the starboard bow. Lovely!

STEERING DOWNWIND is tricky, especially when the wind is exactly astern, as a wobble from the helmsman can cause a gybe. It's extra difficult if there are big waves, as the waves will knock you off course. Practise downwind sailing in light winds so that if you gybe it won't be dangerous!

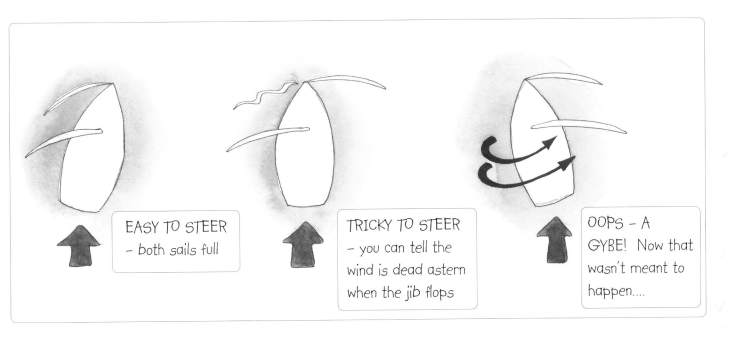

EASY TO STEER – both sails full

TRICKY TO STEER – you can tell the wind is dead astern when the jib flops

OOPS – A GYBE! Now that wasn't meant to happen....

Steering with the wind on the beam is the easiest of all for a beginner. If you go off course a little bit, nothing drastic will happen!

BEAM

BEAM

GETTING A FEEL FOR IT.... When you're more experienced you'll be able to tell whether you're steering to the wind properly by the feel of the boat; if you go off course the trim of the sails will be wrong, she'll lose speed and feel sluggish. Use all your senses, don't just glue your eyes to the wind instruments!

A good helmsman learns to listen to the boat – she'll tell you what she needs!

No – I said turn to PORT!

ENGINE POWER! The basic principles of wheel steering are the same, but motor cruisers handle very differently from sailing yachts. Here are some of the things you need to know....

Motorboat rudders are quite small and they only work when there's plenty of water flowing over them. If the engine is not in gear or the boat is moving very slowly, the wheel alone won't turn the boat - you'll need a burst of engine power.

When any boat turns, the pivot point is towards the front of the boat, so the stern moves further than the bow when you turn the wheel.

TURNING THE WHEEL

A heavy displacement boat will turn gently and slowly but need plenty of space.

A lightweight planing boat will turn fast and easily - but be careful you don't turn the wheel TOO fast!

You and your U turns!

Motor cruisers use the engine controls along with the wheel to manoeuvre the boat in small spaces. Twin screw (two engine) boats have two rudders and use the engine controls to turn the boat in tight spaces, like this....

Pushing the handle forwards makes the engine go forwards - the further you push it, the faster you go. Bring it back to the middle to stop, and backwards to reverse.

A burst of power on the starboard engine will turn the boat to port....

Both engines together will drive the boat straight ahead....

A burst of power on the port engine will turn the boat to starboard.

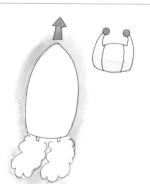

CLOSE TO SHORE there are a lot of things for a helmsman to think about. If you go TOO SLOW you won't be able to manoeuvre the boat - and at slow speeds high sided motor cruisers are easily blown off course by the wind. But if you go TOO FAST you will cause mayhem! Go as slowly and carefully as you can in crowded waters.

This is easy!

Watch your wash, especially if there are people and small boats around. Your wash will be like a tidal wave to a dinghy!

Harbours and rivers have speed limits marked by buoys like this.

Watch out for swimmers, divers, people stepping onto moored yachts or up a mast. When avoiding sailing boats remember they may need to tack, so make allowances for this.

So.. you need more pocket money to pay your speeding fines, do you?

Watch out for mooring buoys - their ropes can get stuck round your propellers and cause a lot of damage to your engine.

HEE HEE!

OUT AT SEA Just because you've got big engines don't think you can ignore the wind! Remember that the wind kicks up big waves which can make steering difficult, especially in a lightweight planing boat. You need to adjust your speed to suit the sea state.

If you're heading into big waves, don't go so fast that you slam into them. Apart from slowing you down, it can damage the boat! If heading directly into the waves gets tricky, try steering a zig zag course between wave crests; this will be easier to steer and easier on the boat.

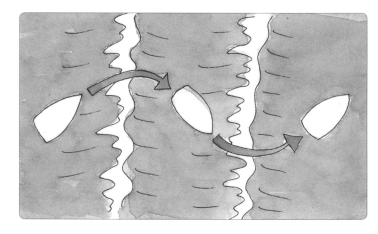

Steering downwind can be fun in gentle waves but when the waves get too big for safety a planing boat will slow down to displacement speed and steer carefully to avoid being rolled over.

Whether you're under sail or power, remember boats don't have brakes!

A planing motor cruiser can be travelling at 30 knots (just over 30 miles per hour) so you'll need to think further ahead than a yacht sailing at 5 knots!

The next chapter tells you what to look out for, how to avoid bumping into anything, and what a good crew needs to do once you're out to sea.

ALL AT SEA

CREW JOB LIST

- Keep a good lookout

- Help to avoid collisions

- Help the navigator

- Write up the log book

- Stay awake on watch

- Stay safe

LOOKOUT! The most important job of the helmsman and crew is to keep a good lookout and avoid bumping into anything! There is a highway code for the sea called the **International Regulations for Preventing Collisions at Sea**. A good crew will know the main rules, starting with this one:

> The first and most important rule is this one:
>
> **"Every vessel shall at all times maintain a proper lookout by sight and hearing as well as by all available means appropriate in the prevailing circumstances...."**
>
> So think like a sailor - stay alert!

Keeping a good lookout may sound easy, but it can be difficult in bad weather! If the boat has a sprayhood up, make sure you can see over the top of it.

An all round lookout means looking behind you occasionally!

How nice to have the sea all to ourselves!

It's not just other boats you need to avoid - look out for floating debris in the water that could damage the boat. Fishing floats like these are common round the coast and difficult to spot, but their lines can get tangled in your propeller!

Remember - all boats have their blind spots! Keep checking them.

Big sails blank out a big area of sea!

How nice to have the sea all to ourselves!

If you're steering from the wheelhouse of a motor cruiser there will be blind spots to the sides, back and under the bow....

Once you've spotted another boat, the next trick is to avoid bumping into it.

First of all work out whether you're on a collision course or not. If you think you are and you're not sure what to do - call the skipper in good time!

How do you know if you're on a collision course? If you're not sure, line up the other boat against a part of your boat, like the shroud or stanchion....

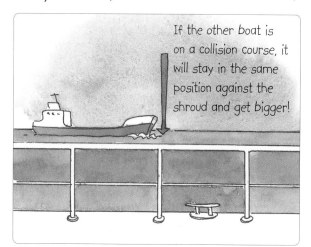

If the other boat is on a collision course, it will stay in the same position against the shroud and get bigger!

.... All clear! This boat is safely moving ahead.

This only works if you keep still! You can also check by lining it up against a compass bearing - if the bearing changes, you're all clear.

What do you do if you are on a collision course? This is what two boats under sail will do....

A boat on PORT TACK gives way to a boat on STARBOARD TACK.

Two boats on the same tack? WINDWARD BOAT gives way to the downwind boat.

These rules apply to sail and power....

POWER boats give way to boats under SAIL (remember a yacht under engine is a power boat).

BUT, there are exceptions....

Big ships can't manoeuvre easily and they also have to stick to deep water channels. Keep out of their way by altering course clearly and in good time.

When two boats under power converge, give way to the vessel approaching from the starboard side.

This boat sees the other one on his starboard bow, so he gives way or slows down.

If two boats under engine meet head on, BOTH boats should turn to starboard (and if you're in a river or narrow channel, drive on the right).

OVERTAKING boats keep well clear of the boat they're overtaking - even if it's a sailing boat overtaking a power boat!

A few more things to look out for when avoiding other boats....

Some boats will show flags or shapes to show why you need to keep out of their way - here are a few of the most common ones.

At night there are lights instead of shapes, but more about those later.

A boat at anchor will show a ball shape like this....

Don't go close to fishing boats flying this shape - their nets can go out a long way!!

The diamond shape means "on tow" - don't try and go through the middle!

This blue and white flag means there are divers in the water.

HOW DO YOU KNOW WHERE YOU ARE? The navigator has the important job of sailing the boat safely from one harbour to another, without bumping into any bits of land on the way. A map for sailors is called a chart, and it contains all the information a navigator needs to know.

Approaching a harbour for the first time, a close up chart like this will show the navigator where to go. Some bigger ports have traffic lights at the entrance, or the skipper may need to call harbour control on the vhf radio to make sure it's safe to enter without getting in the way of big ships.

There may be a close up chart like this on the main chart; the navigator will also have a pilot book with detailed harbour charts and information.

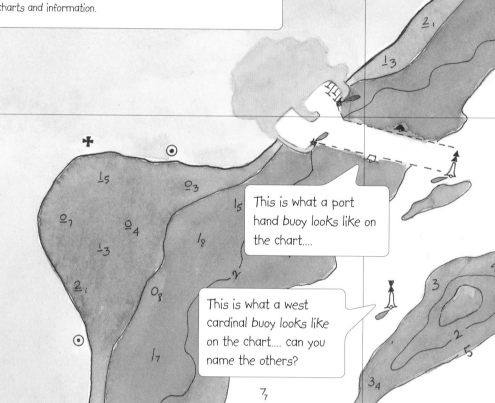

The only land features shown on charts are those that are useful to the sailor - towers, lighthouses, church steeples, large buildings and contours showing high ground.

So WATER TR (conspic) means a conspicuous (very noticeable) water tower.

A ✙ symbol means a church

A ✶ means a light (like a lighthouse)

See how many you can find on your chart.

This is what a port hand buoy looks like on the chart....

This is what a west cardinal buoy looks like on the chart.... can you name the others?

HOW DEEP IS THE WATER? The numbers on the chart (called soundings) show how deep the water would be if the tide was as low as it gets - so there's usually a bit more than the depth shown, depending on the tide. The depths are usually shown in metres - 4 2 means 4.2 metres. The lines are contour lines showing the shape of the sea bed, just like contour lines on land. If the depth has a little line under it, that means it dries out at low tide - so ! 2 means 1.2 metres <u>above</u> the water at low tide. Don't go on this bit!

He knows the way - let's follow him!

The amount of boat sticking down into the water is called its DRAUGHT. A sailing yacht has a deeper draught than a motor cruiser because it has a keel.

An echo sounder tells the sailor how much water is under the keel - keep a careful eye on this when close to shore or in shallow water.

Navigation buoys are important to the sailor - they show where the safer water is, keep you clear of hazards and, because each buoy has its own name, tell you exactly where you are. They have distinctive shapes and colours to help you identify them at a distance. These are the main ones:

CARDINAL BUOYS are black and yellow, and mark dangerous bits.

NORTH CARDINAL
(north of danger
- arrows face up)

EAST CARDINAL
(east of danger
- arrows make an
'E' - sort of!)

WEST CARDINAL
(west of danger
- arrows make a
'W' on its side)

SOUTH CARDINAL
(south of danger -
arrows face down)

LATERAL BUOYS show where the channel is. When approaching harbour leave green ones to starboard and red ones to port (unless they show the deep water channel for big ships, in which case you keep just outside them!)

This is what a starboard hand buoy looks like on the chart....

Make sure the buoy you're looking at really is the one you think it is!

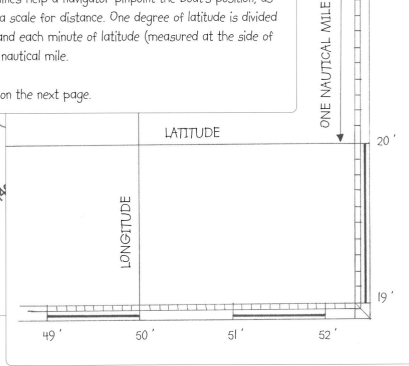

EAST ROCK

There's West Knock - I told you I knew where we were!

This is called a COMPASS ROSE and it helps the navigator to work out which direction he needs to steer. It usually shows both true and magnetic bearings.

What's the difference between 'true' and 'magnetic'? True north is at the north pole; magnetic north wanders around a bit and is a few degrees different. Remember your steering compass gives you MAGNETIC readings.

The straight lines on a chart are LATITUDE (north and south of the equator) and LONGITUDE (east and west of Greenwich meridian). These imaginary lines help a navigator pinpoint the boat's position, as well as providing a scale for distance. One degree of latitude is divided into 60 minutes, and each minute of latitude (measured at the side of the chart) is one nautical mile.

More about this on the next page.

ONE NAUTICAL MILE

21'

LATITUDE

20'

LONGITUDE

19'

49'   50'   51'   52'

What if there's nothing to *see* but sea? Navigators have several tricks up the sleeves of their oilskins, the cleverest of which is gps (global positioning system). A helpful crew will be able to read a position from the gps and enter it into the ship's log....

A gps uses satellites to plot your position and gives it to you in latitude and longitude, which looks like this when written down.

What do the numbers mean? This boat is 51 degrees 55.3 minutes north of the equator, one degree 18 minutes east of the Greenwich meridian. Latitude is always written down first, then longitude. When you learn to navigate you'll be able to work out where this is on the chart.

A gps can also tell you which direction to steer and how far it is to your next waypoint (a waypoint is a buoy or point in your journey which the navigator will have programmed in).

It's clever - but don't forget to look around you as well as at the screen!

We're somewhere here.... sort of....

Until almost the end of the twentieth century sailors didn't have gps to help them. They had to use a combination of skill, maths and *sea sense* to navigate - skills that you'll still need to learn when it's time to skipper your own boat.

Just as important to the navigator is the Ship's Logbook, though this is nothing more technical than paper and pen! The logbook is usually filled in every hour with a record of the boat's course and position. Then if anything goes wrong with the gps the navigator can use the log to work out where you are.

You might not need to fill in all the columns; the skipper will tell you which are most important.

Close to land you will probably use what you can see to show your position; offshore you will use latitude and longitude.

On a motor cruiser there will be space for engine information too.

A proper ship's log like this can be bought from a chandler, but a notebook with columns ruled in it will do just as well - useful if you're on a charter boat.

A crew can also keep their own separate log if they want to - good back up for the navigator, and a great holiday diary.

A family cruising logbook will end up looking a bit like this - but it doesn't matter if it gets covered in doodles and soup stains as long as it gets used properly and the information is clear to read!

As well as useful facts for the navigator, the log book has a page for notes about the voyage. So you can add things you've seen and things that happen, which means you have a great record of your sailing holiday.

Motor cruisers usually get to where they're going much quicker than a yacht. A journey that could take several days under sail can be done in a day in a fast motor cruiser. Navigation is hard to do at high speed so a planing motor cruiser will do its passage planning in advance.

A chart plotter is an electronic chart linked into a gps, so your position shows on the screen, and you can zoom in and out. They're especially useful for boats travelling fast where there is less time to get things wrong!

A motor cruiser will still have a log book and proper charts as a back up - this will probably be filled in every half hour, and may contain simply a list of waypoints, with the time noted as each one is passed as well as course steered and speed.

Both motor cruisers and yachts use an automatic steering system called an autopilot for long trips, which means you don't have to steer by hand all the time.

It's possible for the autopilot to be linked to the gps and chart plotter, but the navigator still needs to keep a keen eye on his position - and the helmsman still needs to keep a sharp lookout for hazards and other ships. A motor cruiser may also have a radar to show up hazards - but this will only help an alert helmsman!

Electronic instruments are only as good as the person using them!

In fast boats, a lot more forward planning is needed! But don't worry, if there's any doubt about your position, the skipper will slow down or stop until he's sorted it out. Sharp eyes for spotting buoys and hazards make you a valuable crew member!

Isn't there a sandbank somewhere round here that we need to look out for?

If your journey is going to take longer than a day, a WATCHKEEPING rota will be used to make sure both crew and boat are looked after. This means waking and sleeping at odd hours, but gives everyone the chance to stay rested, fed and warm.

A watch may last 2, 3 or 4 hours, depending on how many people are on board.

Wrap up well if it's cold on deck - remember to use the heads <u>before</u> you get all your layers on!

It might take a while to adjust to the odd hours, but try to be dressed and ready to go on deck when it's your turn - you'll appreciate this when it's the end of your watch and you're desperate for your bunk!

So what exactly do you do on watch? An experienced crew member will be watch leader; other crew will take turns to steer (unless autopilot is used), fill in the log, trim sails if needed, make hot drinks and above all KEEP WATCH!

The skipper will always be on call if there's anything that happens which needs his attention.

NIGHT SAILING - If your journey is longer than a day, this means sailing through the night, of course.

But how can you keep a good lookout in the dark?

During the day, everything is clear to see......

I know the lens caps are on - I'm practising keeping watch at night!

........but sailing at night turns a familiar coastline into a confusion of lights. How do you make sense of it all? The glow of town lights can make it hard to spot important lights from buoys and ships - and avoid the buoys which aren't lit!

First of all let's have a look at lights that flash but don't move - lighthouses and navigation buoys. Each of these will have its own pattern of flashes per second - if you can count the flashes, you can identify the buoy.

The cardinal buoys are easy to spot - think of the compass as a clock face and you'll remember the pattern.

Green starboard buoys flash green, and red port buoys flash red.

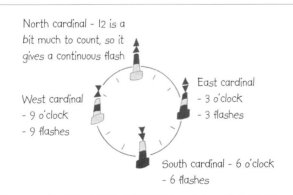

North cardinal - 12 is a bit much to count, so it gives a continuous flash

East cardinal - 3 o'clock - 3 flashes

West cardinal - 9 o'clock - 9 flashes

South cardinal - 6 o'clock - 6 flashes

What do they look like on the chart?

Every buoy with a purple flash by it on the chart is lit up at night - and the sequence of flashes is given like this:

Fl.G(3)10s

This green buoy will give 3 green flashes every ten seconds. Have a look at the chart and see how many you can work out.

How do you make sure you've spotted the right buoy? The most accurate way of timing a light is to use a stop watch but that's not very practical in the dark. Start counting on the first flash - 'one-and-two-and-three' and so on.

Three flashes... Or it could be four... Or maybe five...

On deck, eyes adjust to the dark. If you're in the cabin, keep lights to a minimum so those on watch don't lose their night vision. If there's a red light over the chart table or galley, use this to avoid glare.

If you can *see* a light at *sea* that's moving, it's another boat or ship. You can work out from its lights what it is and which way it's heading, so you Know whether to change course or not. There are many different combinations of ships' lights but it's useful if on watch you can recognise the most common ones. If you can't work out what you're looking at, call the skipper!

These are the simplest and most common ships' lights - you'll find the full range of lights at the back of the Collision regulations book.

 Sailing boat, starboard side (green) and port side (red). Light can be on the bow or on top of the mast.

 Motor boat, starboard side (green) and port side (red).

 A sailing boat with its engine on will have a white light at the top of the mast as well as red or green navigation lights.

 From behind, both yachts and motor boats show a single white light.

 If a boat is coming straight towards you, you will *see* both its red and green lights together, with a white light above if under power.

 Big ships have an extra white light on the bow to help you work out what they are.

A small boat at anchor shows an all round white light; a ship shows two anchor lights.

Always clip on at night, even in a flat calm. If you go over the side, your chances of rescue are slim.

Stay safe, stay warm, stay awake! It can get very cold in an open steering position at night, even with lots of clothes on. Move your arms and legs regularly to Keep warm - this will also Keep you awake!

DREAMBOAT

STAYING SAFE AT SEA - Once you've been at sea for a while, you'll wear your lifejacket and move around the boat safely without thinking about it. But while you're learning, these are some of the things you need to be aware of, starting with sailing yachts....

When using your lifeline, only clip onto bits of the boat that are strong enough! The skipper will show you where these are.

BAD IDEA

jackstay

GOOD IDEA

When do you use a lifeline?

Always at night, but by day it will depend upon the weather - remember, the skipper's word is law!

You may be safe in the cockpit but need to clip on to go forward. Some yachts have webbing lines called jackstays down the side decks to clip onto when going down to the foredeck.

If the boat is heeled over and you need to leave the cockpit, use the uphill side and keep your weight low down, using the handrails.

Some places that are fun to be in calm weather will be off limits when the wind gets stronger!

HOLD ON A MINUTE!
Can you remember which bits of the boat are safe to hold onto? If not, check back to page 16.

Sometimes you need two hands to do a job on deck, like changing sails or using the binoculars.

Try and brace yourself against something secure or hook your arm round the mast or shroud.

Staying safe below decks - you can't fall overboard when you're in the cabin, but you can still hurt yourself if you forget to think like a sailor once you go below....

SAFETY IN THE GALLEY

When making hot drinks, take care and don't fill mugs too full.

Put mugs in the sink to fill them if the boat's moving about.

Always turn the gas off at the tap as well as on the stove when you've finished - the skipper will show you how.

Food can be tricky to prepare (and eat) at sea if the boat is heeled over and bouncing around. Non slip mats are useful.... up to a point!

Put everything away when you've finished with it - or it will end up on the floor! Be especially careful to put sharp objects away.

Think before you hop into your bunk - if the boat tacks, will you fall out? If so, here's what to do....

A LEECLOTH like this will hold you snug, whatever tack you're on! Look for it under your bunk cushion.

Motor cruisers have bigger cabins, safer and less exposed steering positions, and you don't need to go on deck at sea like you do on a sailing yacht. But don't get too relaxed - it's the SPEED and POWER of a motor cruiser that you need to think about....

The foredeck and side decks will be off limits at speed.

A danger point is when the boat accelerates to cruising speed. The skipper will give warning! Make sure you're sitting down or holding on tight.

I said, 'Hold tight, I'm going to accelerate'.

You occasionally use lifelines on some motor cruisers, so make sure you attach the line to a secure point - and not too near the stern as you don't want to get close to the propellers if you do fall in!

The steps up to the flybridge can be tricky at sea - hold tight and always come down like you do on a ladder.

Food can be difficult to prepare on a fast planing boat - your dinner might have to wait until you're safe in harbour.

Cheese and pickle or ham and cucumber.

Cruising, like all adventures, has low points as well as high points. Next we'll have a look at what to do when it's not all plain sailing - when you're scared or seasick and even the skipper is stressed....

PREPARING FOR BAD WEATHER.... The forecast always tells you when bad weather is coming, so cruisers close to shore will have time to take shelter. A motor cruiser with its faster speed is nearly always able to get into harbour before a storm arrives but a sailing boat on passage will make a few preparations and then put up with whatever the weather brings....

A well fed, warm and rested crew will cope with bad weather far better than weak, cold and tired crew. It's a good idea to prepare snacks and flasks of hot drinks in advance as it may be too difficult in rough weather.

Do you want pickle in your cheese and banana sandwich, Dad?

Bad weather can change your plans. The skipper may head for a different, safer harbour, or he may decide to stay out at sea. Deeper water with regular waves can be safer in a gale than being too close to land.

You can open your eyes, now, we're in!

A boat will keep well clear of a lee shore (a downwind shore) - even if there is a harbour, it could be too dangerous to enter!

As the wind gets stronger, the boat will be reefed. This means making the sails smaller so that you stay in control and nothing breaks. If you're asked to take the helm while a reef is taken in, try to hold the boat almost into the wind.

You need to be particularly strict about wearing your lifejacket and harness in bad weather.

Yes, I know Ellen MacArthur had much bigger waves than this, and no, it doesn't make me feel any better!

Sometimes conditions below deck can be worse than on deck, because loose things go flying, the motion seems extreme and the noise of the boat slamming into waves seems very loud.

If it's possible to go on deck, wrap up well and watch the way the boat rides the waves. All that wild motion will make more sense, and you'll be a lot less scared. Boats are built for waves, they know exactly what to do!

STRESSED SKIPPERS AND TRICKY SITUATIONS - When things get difficult, the skipper has to put the boat first. If you're being ignored - or being shouted at - it's because something urgent is going on and there's no time to explain or say please!

Don't get upset if you're being ignored - it just means that the boat needs the skipper's urgent attention!

Seasickness is horrible, but you can learn to cope with it and look after yourself. If it's too rough to be on deck, go to bed and stay lying down. Usually seasickness only lasts a few days until you get your 'sea legs'.

Just think - when you're a bit more experienced you'll be up there on deck battling with the storm instead of lying in a nice warm bunk!

It's not just bad weather and gear failure that makes a skipper stressed. Tricky pilotage, like finding the safe route into a rock strewn harbour, can cause tense moments.

You can help by using your sharp eyes to spot buoys and landmarks, or reading out instructions from the pilot book. Or go below and tidy up the cabin ready for harbour.

But it's not all drama on the high seas! On a long passage there can be boring bits too, so here's some advice from experienced young sailors on things to do when there's nothing to see but sea....

I spy with my little eye, something beginning with S....

Board games
(as long as they don't have too many bits to get lost) Card games are great - learn some card tricks too!

Puzzle books and quiz books are good - keep plenty of pens and pencils on board.

Listen to music or watch DVDs (take plenty of spare batteries!)

Drawing - keep a sketch book, or make a cruising diary by filling in your own log book.

Practise knot tying - the important ones are in Chapter Six. Then try the turk's head in Chapter Eight or other decorative knots.

Reading - get stuck into a good story or look up reference books for wildlife or the harbours you're visiting.

Are we nearly there yet?

SEA SENSE

There's more to cruising than making the boat go. A good sailor has all kinds of knowledge about weather, tides, knots and seamanship as well as an understanding and respect for the sea.

CREW JOB LIST

- Understand the weather forecast

- Read the tide tables

- Tie knots that work

- Understand flags and ensigns

- Look after the sea!

WEATHER BASICS - Even a landlubber can appreciate how important the weather is to the sailor. If the skipper is listening to the shipping forecast, don't even think about interrupting! A forecast can make the difference between a sunny day on the water with a picnic on the beach or a boring day gale bound in harbour. So what does it all mean?

As well as harbour and marina offices, you can get a forecast from the internet, telephone, TV, Radio Shipping Forecast, weatherfax, or from the coastguard who will broadcast at certain times through vhf/dsc radio.

> Huh.....???????

> So.... the low over the North Sea is declining and high pressure building from the Atlantic... and we all know what that means, don't we!

Sailors need to be patient. Try not to be too disappointed if the forecast means you can't sail today.

> !@!*!*

> Oh dear, must be a bad forecast again....

THE HIGHS AND LOWS OF A FORECAST

A weather map is called a SYNOPTIC CHART and it shows areas of high and low pressure. The lines work like contours of a map where the closer the contours, the steeper the slope. On a weather chart the closer the contours (called ISOBARS), the stronger the wind.

LOW PRESSURE systems are called DEPRESSIONS. The wind travels round them anticlockwise in the northern hemisphere, clockwise in the southern hemisphere. Low pressure usually brings unsettled weather with the rain and wind.

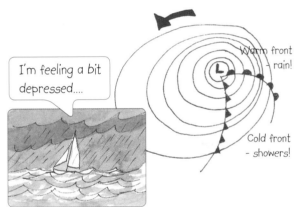

> I'm feeling a bit depressed....

Warm front - rain!

Cold front - showers!

HIGH PRESSURE SYSTEMS, called ANTICYCLONES, usually bring settled, clear, weather and light winds. The wind travels round them clockwise in the northern hemisphere, anticlockwise in the southern hemisphere.

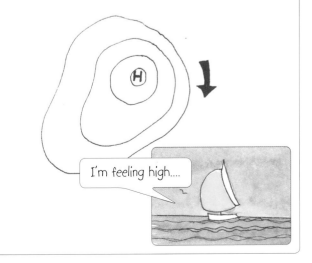

> I'm feeling high....

How do you understand the forecast? First of all the general synopsis tells you what the lows and highs are doing, then each sea area is covered. The shipping forecast is much more detailed than the general forecast, and each word in it means something exact....

These are the sea areas around North Europe and Britain - do you know which one you're sailing in?

When listening to the forecast, write down not just your area but the ones around it so that you get a better all round picture.

'rain or showers'
- this bit tells you whether it will rain, snow, or stay fair.

'....Wight, Portland, Plymouth, southwest 4-5 veering west or northwest 6 to gale 8 later, rain or showers, good becoming moderate or poor....'

'gale 8 later'
means you have up to 12 hours to get to a safe harbour! IMMINENT means within six hours, SOON means six to 12 hours, LATER means after 12 hours.

'good becoming moderate or poor'
- this bit is about visibility, which is as important to the sailor as wind.

'southwest 4-5 veering west'
This is the wind direction and strength - more about the wind on the next page. Veering means the wind is changing in a clockwise direction (eg. a northerly changing to an easterly). Backing means anticlockwise (eg. changing from east to north).

Wind strength is measured using the Beaufort Scale, devised in the 17th century by Admiral Beaufort, who based it on observations of the wind and waves.

Hmm... is it windy, very windy or very very windy?

These days we have wind instruments to measure the exact speed of the wind - practise working out what force you think the wind is, then check on the boat's instruments to see if you got it right!

Wind direction is shown by which point of the compass a wind is blowing from (a north wind blows <u>from</u> the north, not <u>to</u> the north!)

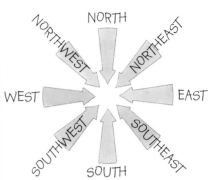

THE BEAUFORT SCALE

(a knot is a nautical mile per hour)

Force 1	Light airs (1-3 knots)
Force 2	Light breeze (4-6 knots)
Force 3	Gentle breeze (7-10 knots)
Force 4	Moderate breeze (11-16 knots)
Force 5	Fresh breeze (17-21 knots)
Force 6	Strong breeze (22-27 knots)
Force 7	Near gale (28-33 knots)
Force 8	Gale (34-40 knots)
Force 9	Severe gale (41-47 knots)
Force 10	Storm (48-55 knots)
Force 11	Violent Storm (56-63 knots)
Force 12	Hurricane (over 64 knots)

Gentle winds mean fast planing conditions for motor cruisers and slow sailing for yachts.

..... at force 3, everyone's happy - yachts will have all their sails up and motor cruisers are able to go fast as the waves are still quite small....

..... by force 4 and 5, yachts are sailing fast and beginning to reef down (make the sails smaller), while motor cruisers are slowing down to displacement speed. Waves are getting bigger with white crests....

As the wind strengthens to a gale, yachts are well reefed down and motor cruisers are steering slowly and carefully through the breaking waves - uncomfortable but manageable!

You're unlikely to be out above force 8 unless you're on a long passage in a well-prepared boat which will be able to stay safe at sea!

OTHER KINDS OF WEATHER.... Different parts of the world have different weather patterns, so if you're going abroad on a charter holiday, there will be new things to learn! World weather patterns will affect you if you're crossing an ocean, but if you're sailing closer to shore there may be local effects to think about.

SEA BREEZES

Sea breezes happen near coasts in hot, settled weather. They spring up about lunchtime and die down at tea time. Here's why -

Land warms up faster than sea, so as the warm air over land rises, cooler air is drawn in from the sea to replace it. By the end of the day the temperature of land and sea have equalled out and the cycle stops.

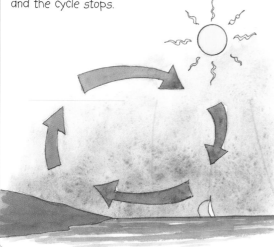

LOCAL WINDS

If there are mountains near the coast, these will have an effect on the weather. The Mediterranean is well known for sudden strong winds blowing down from the mountains, and they all have names - like the Mistral in Southern France, the Meltemi in Greece and the Scirocco which blows from the deserts of North Africa (hot, dry and full of sand!)

cough! splutter!

HOW CAN YOU TELL IF THERE'S BAD WEATHER COMING?

'When the glass falls low, prepare for a blow

When it rises high, let all your kites fly'

Don't wait for the experts to tell you what the weather is doing - most boats have a barometer on board which measures air pressure. Low pressure means a depression is coming, high pressure means settled weather. If the pressure changes very quickly, strong winds are coming.

There are two pointers on the dial - one measures the pressure and the other can be moved by hand. Twiddle the button in the middle to make the two pointers line up - then when you next take a look you can see how far and how quickly the pressure has risen or fallen.

There's a column in the ship's log to record the barometer reading; impress your skipper and put it in when you fill out the log!

ALL ABOUT TIDES - If you sail in tidal waters, you'll need to understand how they affect you. The navigator or skipper will do all the tidal calculations, but it's useful if the crew understands the basics and can read a tide table.

HOW DO TIDES WORK? (A bit of science) Tides are caused by the pull of the sun and moon on the oceans. Twice a month the sun, earth and moon are in line which causes SPRING TIDE. By the time of half moon the pull has weakened and this is called NEAP TIDE.

SPRING TIDES, at new moon and full moon, have the strongest pull.

NEAP TIDES happen at half moon and are not as strong as spring tides.

HOW TO READ TIDE TABLES....

The tide goes in and out twice a day, so there are usually two high tides and two low tides each day. The falling tide is called the EBB and the rising tide is called the FLOOD.

TIDE TABLES can tell you the times of high and low water each day as well as the height of tide above chart datum for each tide....

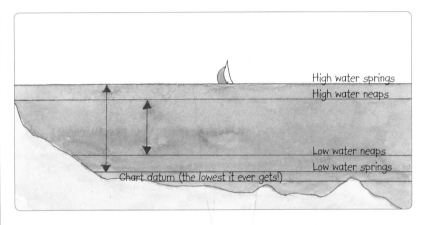

High water springs
High water neaps
Low water neaps
Low water springs
Chart datum (the lowest it ever gets!)

16	0043	4.5
Tu	0715	2.0
	1316	4.6
	1957	1.8

This tells us that the first high tide of the day is 43 minutes past midnight with 4.5 metres above chart datum, dropping to 2 metres above chart datum at low tide at 7.15 in the morning. Got it?

Two more things to think about -

Tide times are different round the coast. Use the right tables for the harbour you're in! Times may need to be adjusted for Summer Time - if they do, there will be a note at the bottom of the page.

Complicated? Cruising is about using your brains as well as your body!

If this happens on sand or mud you just have to wait for the tide to come back in.

If it happens on rocks, or in bad weather, it can be dangerous! Navigators always make allowances for the tide.

That's the last time I let you do the navigation!

EBBTIDE

Tides can be useful, too. You will often see a yacht dried out against a harbour wall or posts to do repairs or clean the bottom - but you have to get the job done before the tide comes back in!

It's not just the rise and fall of tides that matter to the sailor, it's the tidal stream - the direction the tide is flowing. Around coasts with a strong tidal stream, the skipper of a sailing boat will plan to travel with the tide rather than against it (even if it means leaving in the middle of the night!) Spring tides run faster than neap tides, remember, as there is more water to shift!

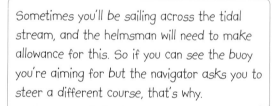

The navigator uses the chart or a Tidal Atlas to show him what the tidal stream is doing and how it changes hour by hour.

You can't see how the tide is moving until it flows past a fixed object like a buoy.

A motor cruiser has different priorities. His faster speed means that he doesn't have to wait for a fair tide - in fact, he may choose to travel against the tide. This is because the sea is smoother when wind and tide are moving in the same direction.

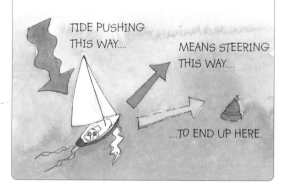

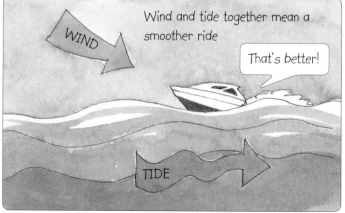

KNOTS - You learnt how to tie a round turn and two half hitches when tying on fenders, so now it's time to get to know a few more important knots a sailor needs. It's important to use the right knot for the right job - and tie it properly! These are the ones you're most likely to need, so keep some spare ropes handy to practise on.

BOWLINE

This makes a loop in a rope, useful for tying a sheet onto the clew of a sail, or looping a mooring line round a bollard. It's quite tricky to learn, so have a go....

   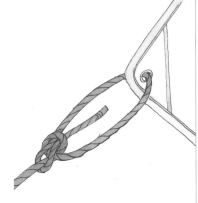

FIGURE OF EIGHT KNOT

This one's easy to learn - tie it at the end of sheets to stop them pulling through a block....

REEF KNOT

For tying reef points in a sail - you'll use this one most for tying up sail ties.

CLOVE HITCH

A quick and easy way of tying a rope to a post or rail....

SINGLE AND DOUBLE SHEET BEND

These are used to tie two lengths of rope together, for example if you want to make an extra mooring line. Use a single sheet bend if your two pieces of rope are the same type and thickness, but if they're are different, it's important to put an extra tuck in and make a double sheet bend.

SINGLE
SHEET
BEND

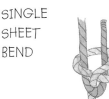  

DOUBLE
SHEET
BEND

FLAGS AND ENSIGNS - For centuries, flags have been used to send signals between boats, and they always mean something exact. You don't need to learn the flag signal alphabet any more (unless you want to just for fun), but some flags are still used. Here are some that you'll see.

ENSIGNS

Ensigns are flown from the stern of the ship and show you which country she comes from. There are three types of British ensign, red, white and blue....

On most British boats you'll see a red ensign like this.

This means that the skipper belongs to a yacht club with special permission to fly a blue ensign which may have an emblem on it. The yacht must wear the matching burgee.

This one is very special - it's for the Royal Yacht Squadron and Royal Navy only.

When do you fly the ensign? In harbour, between 8am and sunset. It's the crew's job to remember to take the ensign down at sunset and put it away. When out at sea, it's usual to leave it up the whole time you're on passage but you can take it down overnight if you want to.

RACING YACHTS

A yacht in a race doesn't fly an ensign or burgee; instead it has a code flag on the backstay to represent the class it's racing in.

BURGEES

Every yacht club has its own flag called a burgee, which is usually flown from the top of the mast.

"Muddy Bottom Yacht Club'

COURTESY FLAGS

When you sail to another country it's usual to fly a small flag of the country you're visiting. On a yacht, you'll find a special flag halyard on the starboard side of the boat; a motor cruiser usually has a small mast or flagstaff to fly them from.

BIENVENUE À CALAIS

Er.... Skipper, you know you told me to put the Dutch courtesy flag up....

HOUSE FLAGS

These are flags that a boat might fly to show regattas or rallies that it's been to, or it can be an individual boat flag designed by the crew. Why not design a house flag for your family or your boat?

....they've gone below to design a really nice house flag

OK, if you've finished the skull now put it in the cutlasses....

SIGNAL FLAGS

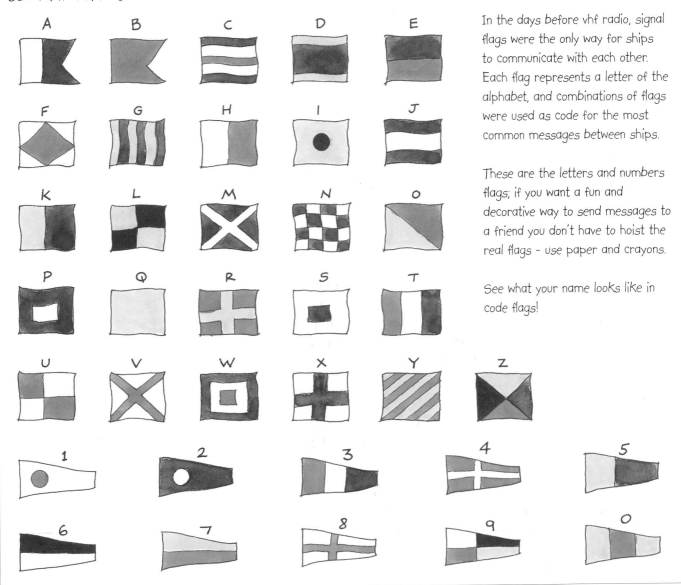

In the days before vhf radio, signal flags were the only way for ships to communicate with each other. Each flag represents a letter of the alphabet, and combinations of flags were used as code for the most common messages between ships.

These are the letters and numbers flags; if you want a fun and decorative way to send messages to a friend you don't have to hoist the real flags - use paper and crayons.

See what your name looks like in code flags!

DRESSING OVERALL

The most common use for signal flags now is for special occasions like regattas, when you fly them all in a row like this. A harbour full of boats dressed overall looks very colourful. You have to take them down when you get under way, though!

Dressed overall

Undressed overall!

SIGNALS IN USE TODAY

Some flag signals you might see today are these....

Fly the 'Q' flag from the port side, opposite the courtesy flag, when you're arriving at a foreign country. This tells the Customs and Excise that you've arrived from another country and they need to pay you a visit. You don't need to use the 'Q' flag between European countries.

A big ship being helped into a harbour by a pilot should show the 'H' flag.

If you see a boat flying the 'A' flag, it means she is a dive boat and you should keep well clear as there could be divers in the water.

RESPECT FOR THE SEA - A good sailor will look after the sea and never take it for granted. The sea supports a huge variety of life - an estimated 10 million species! The oceans cover about 70% of the planet's surface and sea pollution is a big threat.

So how can one small sailor help? For a start, avoiding throwing rubbish overboard. You might think it doesn't matter far out to sea but it does. Did you know that a tin can will last 50 years under water and a glass bottle 1,000 years? And plastic wrapping does huge damage to wildlife.

WILDLIFE AT SEA

Keep reference books on board to help you identify seabirds and sea creatures. Every boat will have a pair of binoculars, or better still, take your own pair.

There will also be plenty of wildlife to spot close to shore, once you're in harbour and start exploring all those beaches, rivers and creeks.

Don't be silly, of course there aren't any whales round here!

It's exciting to spot marine mammals like dolphins and porpoises, especially when they come and play with you by swimming alongside the boat.

How do you know whether you've spotted a dolphin or a porpoise? There are many different types of both, but generally a dolphin has more of a beak than a porpoise, as well as a higher dorsal fin.

COMMON DOLPHIN

HARBOUR PORPOISE

The Whale and Dolphin Conservation Society is always interested to hear about when and where sea mammals are seen in European waters. You can download a sightings form from their website www.wdcs.org.uk - taking photos will help you identify what you've seen.

LAND HO!

Making landfall is exciting when you've been at sea all day - it's even more exciting when you've been at sea for weeks! You still need to think like a sailor when you're in harbour, helping to moor the boat, getting ashore and using the dinghy safely.

> ### CREW JOB LIST
>
> - Help take down and stow sails
>
> - Help with mooring lines and fenders
>
> - Use the dinghy sensibly

Approaching harbour, be ready when the skipper gives the order to lower sails. To take the mainsail down the boat will need to head into the wind, but a jib can be lowered or rolled in any time. This is what you can do to help....

LOWERING THE MAIN

The first job is to tighten the topping lift to take the weight of the boom once the sail is down. It is sometimes useful to release the kicker and ease the mainsheet first. Then the halyard is released gently, and the sail pulled down....

Topping lift tight...

sail is pulled down....

as the halyard is released.

Sail ties ready (tied on so they don't blow away)

Make sure the halyard has a turn around a winch or cleat.

A roller furling jib is quick and easy to take in. One person keeps a bit of tension on the sheet and eases it out gently while the control line is pulled in.

When the jib is in, the control line is cleated off and the sheets left tight.

STOWING THE MAIN

Once the sail is down, it will need tidying up into folds then tying up with sail ties. Remember how to do a reef knot? If the sail tie is long enough, you can leave a loop in the final tie like you do on a shoelace.

LOWERING THE JIB

The halyard on a hanked on jib will be gently lowered while the sail is gathered in quickly to stop the wind filling it and blowing it over the side.

Once the jib is down, unclip the halyard carefully...

- don't let go of it!

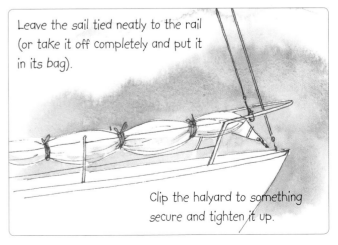

Leave the sail tied neatly to the rail (or take it off completely and put it in its bag).

Clip the halyard to something secure and tighten it up.

If you're coming into a marina, harbour, or alongside another boat, you'll need to get mooring lines (also called 'warps') and fenders ready....

GETTING WARPS AND FENDERS READY

Make sure mooring lines are tied on securely (can you remember how? If not, check back to page 22). You may need to put warps and fenders on both sides of the boat if you're not sure which side you're going to be.

The mooring line should be tied to the cleat, led through the fairlead, round the outside of the guardrail and coiled ready to take ashore.

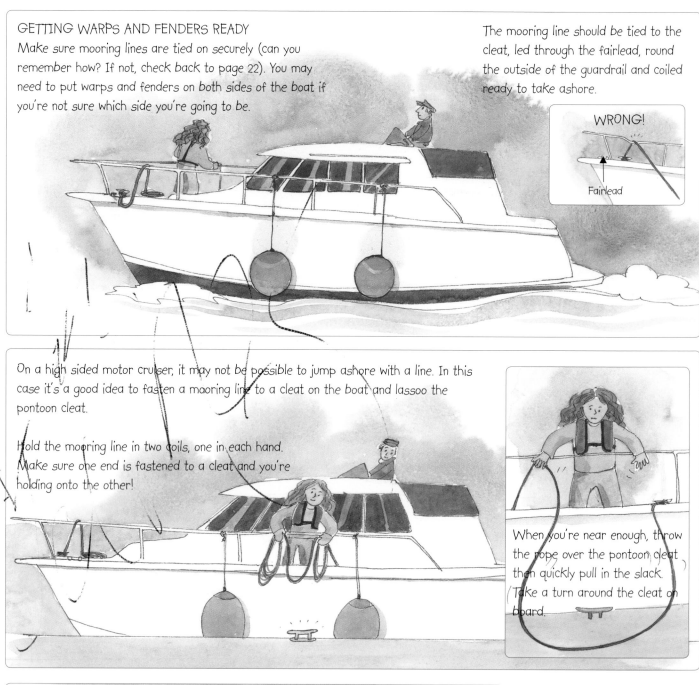

WRONG!

Fairlead

On a high sided motor cruiser, it may not be possible to jump ashore with a line. In this case it's a good idea to fasten a mooring line to a cleat on the boat and lassoo the pontoon cleat.

Hold the mooring line in two coils, one in each hand. Make sure one end is fastened to a cleat and you're holding onto the other!

When you're near enough, throw the rope over the pontoon cleat then quickly pull in the slack. Take a turn around the cleat on board.

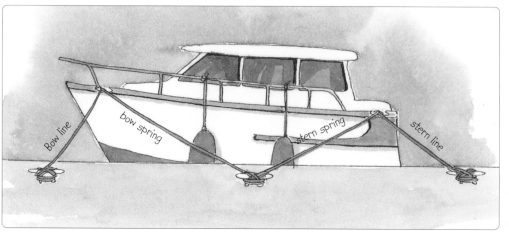

Bow line

bow spring

stern spring

stern line

Once the boat is secure, the fenders may need to be adjusted and the mooring lines will be arranged like this. Bow and stern lines hold the boat into the pontoon, and the springs stop it moving forwards or backwards.

Coming alongside in a yacht, the best place to stand is by the shrouds, which give you something secure to hold onto.

Hold the mooring line in a coil - check it's not tangled or caught on anything.

Make sure it's through the fairlead and outside the guardrail!

It's important to WAIT until you can step ashore easily - don't do a flying leap....

As soon as you're ashore, hook the rope round a cleat where the front of the boat will end up. Cleat it off and <u>then help with the other lines.</u>

Taking a turn around a cleat

If you don't take a turn round a cleat and the boat is still moving, you won't be able to hold it. Don't try this!

Once the boat has stopped, cleat off the mooring line quickly and see if you can help secure the other lines.

CLEATED ROPE - don't leave the tail trailing for someone to trip over

HOW DO YOU TIE A MOORING LINE?
The skipper might like you to tie a bowline through the cleat, especially if the boat is going to be left unattended. If you cleat off in the usual way (if you've forgotten how check back to page 20), make sure you don't leave a loose end trailing for people to trip over.

BOWLINE through a cleat - check page 69 if you can't remember how to tie one.

THROWING A LINE If you're lucky enough to find someone on the pontoon to take a line for you, it saves having to jump ashore. To throw a line without it tangling or falling in the water, divide the rope into two coils with slack in between. Throw the first coil immediately followed by the second.... but don't forget to make sure the end of the rope is securely fastened to the boat!

I've thrown the line, Dad – what next?

In busy harbours and marinas, you sometimes have to tie alongside another boat. This is called rafting up, and your mooring lines are tied up to the boat next door as well as extra lines ashore. It can take a while to get ashore when you're in a raft up! Cross at the widest point of each boat then walk round the foredeck. Be as quiet as you can!

Be careful crossing from boat to boat especially if one is higher than the other. In a tidal harbour at low tide there may also be a steep ladder up to the quay!

RAFT UP RULES

Always walk across the foredeck of each boat. Don't clomp! If your shoes are muddy, take them off.

If there's someone in the cockpit, ask politely if you can cross their boat.

Be as quiet as you can - especially at night.

Respect privacy - don't peep down other people's hatches, even if they're open!

PICKING UP A MOORING - The helmsman will approach the buoy in the same direction as the other moored boats - into tide or wind - which will help him to slow down and stop. If your job is to go on the foredeck and pick up the mooring buoy, here's what to do....

The skipper won't be able to see the buoy as you approach.

Use the boathook to point to the buoy and call out the distance.

Scoop up the rope attached to the pickup buoy and shout to the helmsman when you've got it safe on board.

If there isn't a pickup buoy there could just be a looped rope like this.

If there is no pickup buoy and no rope on the mooring, you'll need to hook it with the boathook and thread your own rope through it - a job for two people as the buoy will be heavy to hold onto.

If you can't reach the buoy, don't stretch too far and risk ending up in the water! If you miss, the skipper will have another go.

I've got it, Dad!

Finally, secure the rope by hooking it over a cleat.

Make sure the rope goes through the bow roller or a fairlead.

ANCHORING   Handling anchors is tricky work, although it's easier if the boat has an electric windlass (anchor winch). This is how it's done....

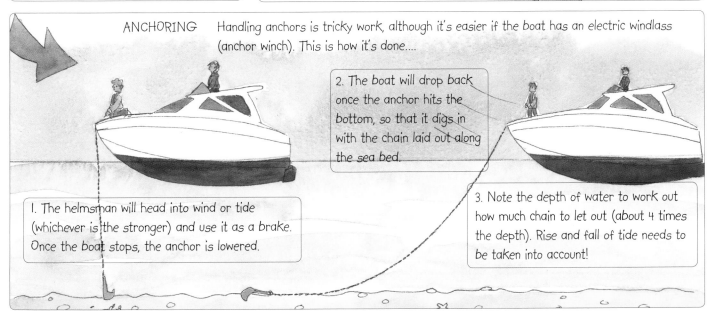

2. The boat will drop back once the anchor hits the bottom, so that it digs in with the chain laid out along the sea bed.

1. The helmsman will head into wind or tide (whichever is the stronger) and use it as a brake. Once the boat stops, the anchor is lowered.

3. Note the depth of water to work out how much chain to let out (about 4 times the depth). Rise and fall of tide needs to be taken into account!

USING THE DINGHY - If you're on a mooring or at anchor, you'll need the dinghy to get ashore. Surprisingly, more accidents happen in the dinghy between the yacht and the shore than out at sea - because it's easy to stop thinking like a sailor when the anchor goes down! Always let someone know where you are going and when you'll be back, and never get into a dinghy without wearing your lifejacket or buoyancy aid.

There are two types of dinghy - inflatable or rigid - and both can be used with oars or outboard engine. Inflatables are easy to store on a small cruiser and need blowing up with a foot pump. A large yacht or motor cruiser may carry a rigid dinghy on deck, but on smaller boats it can be towed astern for short trips. Here are some of the things you need to carry with you....

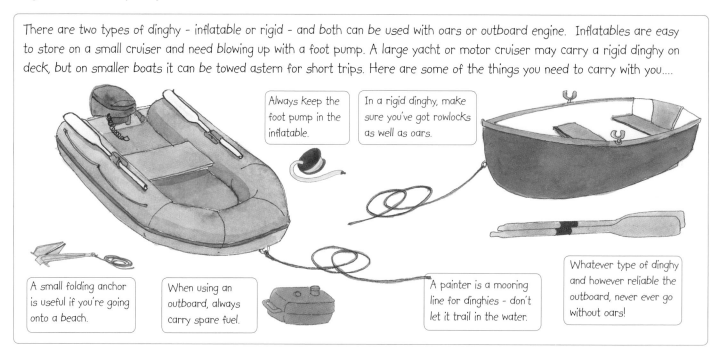

Always keep the foot pump in the inflatable.

In a rigid dinghy, make sure you've got rowlocks as well as oars.

A small folding anchor is useful if you're going onto a beach.

When using an outboard, always carry spare fuel.

A painter is a mooring line for dinghies - don't let it trail in the water.

Whatever type of dinghy and however reliable the outboard, never ever go without oars!

Small dinghies are wobbly - especially inflatables which are a bit squidgy as well. This can take you by surprise when you've got used to the relatively stable motion of the bigger boat.

Wait for...

me!

Step down backwards, holding onto something secure. Step into the middle of the dinghy not the edge!

Try to load the dinghy so that the weight is evenly balanced....

Don't overload! Do two trips if necessary.

HOW TO ROW Everyone needs to learn to row. Even the *best* outboard engines go wrong sometimes, and there are all Kinds of things you can do with oars that you can't do with an engine.

You'll spot more wildlife under oars as it's totally quiet, and you can get further up a creek than you can with an outboard - but remember to check your tides!

LEARN TO ROW in calm water with no strong tides. Make small circles with your hands - out at the top, in at the bottom. Get into a rhythm and if you get in a muddle, stop, lift your oars parallel with the water and try again.

Row with your right hand oar only to turn to starboard, and left hand oar to turn to port.

To row faster, lean back with your whole body as you pull with your hands. Keep your circles small - if your blade digs too deep into the water it will be hard to pull out again!

Look over your shoulder regularly so you don't bump into anything! You need to give way to boats under sail; watch out for swimmers too.

Remember to sit facing the stern of the dinghy

COMING ALONGSIDE - Use the wind or tide as your *brake*, whichever is the stronger. If there's a bathing platform at the stern, that may *be* the easiest place to get on *board*; if not, come to the side.

Approach gently at an angle and pull your inside oar in. A quick *backward* stroke of the outside oar will bring you alongside.

Step up carefully from the middle of the dinghy - bring the painter with you and tie it off as soon as you're on board.

Stow the oars safely in the bottom of the dinghy.

ROWING IN SAFETY - Rowing is slow - normally this is not a problem but if there's a strong tide or wind, it can make life difficult. Tides can be particularly strong in a river, so if you're swept downtide of your boat, get into shallow water where the tides are weaker.

You should then be able to row uptide past your boat so that when you get back into the strong tide it carries you down onto it.

Rowing at 2 Knots....

against a tide of 3 Knots = going backwards!

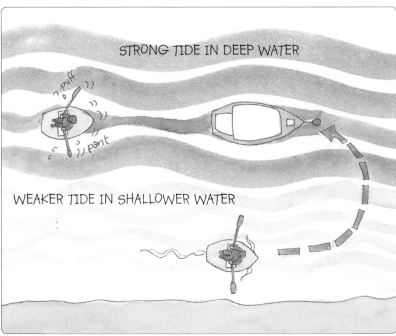

STRONG TIDE IN DEEP WATER

WEAKER TIDE IN SHALLOWER WATER

If the wind is too strong to row against - particularly a problem with lightweight inflatable dinghies - get into shallow water if you can, and pull the dinghy upwind of where you want to go.

This only works on firm sand - don't try it on a soft muddy shore!

If the tide is sideways on to the way you want to go, head up into it to compensate. It helps to line up two objects on shore to help you keep on track.

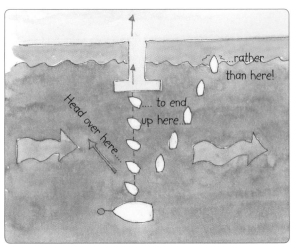

...rather than here!

.... to end up here...

Head over here....

If you lose an oar, don't lean out too far to reach it or you'll end up in the water....

Use the remaining oar like a paddle to go after your oar or get you to safety.

For longer dinghy trips, and when there are strong tides or winds an outboard engine makes life a lot easier! Let's look next at how to handle a dinghy under engine....

Twist the throttle to adjust the speed

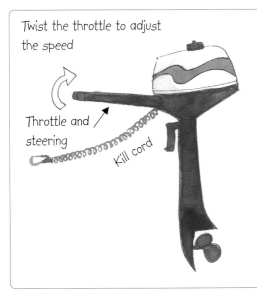

Throttle and steering

Kill cord

A small outboard engine is steered with a short tiller that turns the whole engine. It takes a bit of getting used to as it's easy to turn the tiller too far - you only need very slight movements to change direction. You also have to get used to twisting the throttle to change speed!

Practise at very slow speeds to get the hang of it. Make sure you always carry enough fuel (and take a pair of oars, of course!)

If the engine has a kill cord, attach this to your lifejacket. This will stop the engine instantly if you fall over the side.

Cut the engine and tilt it forwards in good time when coming to a shallow shore. Don't risk damaging the propeller!

When leaving shore, row or wade out into deeper water before starting the engine.

Going fast with an outboard engine is great fun - but there are lots of reasons why it's often a really bad idea. In a busy anchorage a small dinghy creates a big wash which is not just unpleasant for others around but can be dangerous. Think what would happen if your wash caused a yacht to rock when someone was pouring hot water in the galley, or stepping into their dinghy. Give other boats and swimmers a wide berth.

Good seamanship means thinking ahead and using your imagination!

WHEEE!

I'm wild!

Wildlife can get stressed by your speed too....

Going too fast is not just a danger to other people – it is very easy at speed for an inflatable to flip over!

AVOIDING OTHER BOATS -
Whether you're under oars, outboard or sail, never cross an anchored or moored boat at the bows - remember that moored or anchored boats are held downwind or down tide. That same wind or tide will affect you too and you'll be blown or pulled down onto the bow. Aim at the stern and let the wind or tide pull you clear.

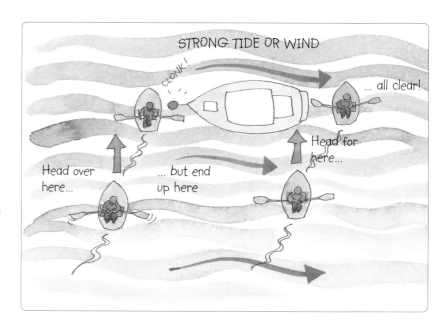

Once you've taken on board all the safety issues about dinghies and harbours, you can have a whole lot of fun, especially in hot weather. Swimming, beachcombing, exploring and eating barbecued sausages covered in sand are all part of the unique cruising experience!

If you're swimming from the boat, it's a good idea to float a fender on a long line astern, so you can grab onto it and pull yourself back to the boat if you get tired.

Tides are always stronger in deeper water - check the tide before you dive over the side!

In hot weather the dinghy can make a great paddling pool to help you cool off!

If you have a barbecue ashore, make sure you leave the beach exactly as you found it and take all your rubbish back to the boat.

If your cruiser has room for a sailing dinghy, you can have even more fun exploring the places that big boats can't get to!

Think about what the tide is doing when you pull the dinghy up the beach - use the anchor if there's nowhere to tie the painter.

BAGGYWRINKLES!

What on earth is baggywrinkle?

On traditional sailing ships baggywrinkle is made from lots of loose ends of old rope woven together and wound round the rigging at places where the sail rubs against it, to protect the sail from chafe.

This chapter is full of loose ends – not made of rope but with lots of interesting facts that a sailor might like to know. Some are really useful, some are just curious; so save this chapter for when you're on a really long boring passage or storm bound in harbour with nowhere to go!

It's your fault for telling the Captain we were at a loose end!

Which sea words are used in everyday language?

There are more sea words in day to day language than you might think.

Lots of people talk about **taking a different tack** when they want to try a new approach to something and have you ever been **taken aback?** This means being surprised or stopped short. When a sailing boat catches the wind on the wrong side of the sails, it stops suddenly – the sails are said to be backed, so the boat is 'taken aback'.

TAKEN ABACK

What about **touch and go?** This means uncertainty whether something will succeed or not ('It was touch and go whether he'd make it').

One explanation for this phrase comes from the east coast sailing barges which often had to tack up narrow rivers with their heavy cargoes. Instead of keels the barges have leeboards on either side which can be raised or lowered – so when the leeboard touches the mudbank it's time to go about – touch and go.

TOUCH AND GO

squelch!

Sorry – did you say go about?

IN THE DOLDRUMS

I'm bored!

Have you heard anyone say they're in the **Doldrums?** This means they're bored or feel their life is not going anywhere.

The real doldrums are a band of light winds around the equator where sailing ships can sometimes get becalmed for weeks on end.

See if you can find any other sailing terms in everyday language - but don't make **heavy weather** of it!

Where do the words PORT and STARBOARD come from?

Before rudders were invented, ships were steered with a long oar lashed to the side of the boat at the stern. This steering oar was always on the right hand side of the boat, presumably because most people are right handed, so this side became known as the STEERING BOARD or STARBOARD side. The other side became the PORT side because this was the side the ship tied up to the quay, to avoid damaging the steering oar.

No, silly, fenders go on the PORT side!

STEERING OAR

What is the phonetic alphabet?

Now this is a really useful one – learn this and practise it with your friends. It's used on the vhf radio when you're spelling something out and want to make sure there's no mistake. Don't wait until you're qualified to use the vhf, learn the alphabet now – it will also come in useful if you're trying to spell something over the phone!

A alpha	J juliet	S sierra	
B bravo	K kilo	T tango	
C charlie	L lima	U uniform	
D delta	M mike	V victor	
E echo	N november	W whiskey	
F foxtrot	O oscar	X x ray	
G golf	P papa	Y yankee	
H hotel	Q quebec	Z zulu	
I india	R romeo		

In an emergency you need to be able to spell the name of your boat by phonetic alphabet. Practise your boat name until you can do it without thinking.

Why is a pirate flag called the Jolly Roger?

One story that explains why the skull and crossbones flag is called the Jolly Roger concerns a Welsh pirate called Bartholomew Roberts or Black Bart. He was an unusual pirate - as well as being very religious, (his men were not allowed to fight on a Sunday!), he did not allow any alcohol on his ship.

Black Bart loved fine clothes and his favourite outfit was a bright red jacket, silk stockings and ostrich feather in his hat! Because of this, the French members of his crew started calling him Le Jolie Rouge ('pretty red') which gradually changed into Jolly Roger, a name that stuck for both the pirate and his skull and crossbones flag.

Yo ho ho and a nice cup of tea!

What is the Crossing the Line Ceremony?

Crossing the equator by sea has always been celebrated on board, a tradition that continues to this day. Whether you're on a racing yacht or an ocean liner, you'll find some kind of ceremony taking place.

So now you're telling me I have to wash this lot off in salt water!

Those who have 'crossed the line' before dress up as King Neptune and his court, then each person on board who's never crossed the line before is brought before King Neptune and made to do crazy things – usually involving cold porridge, lots of mess and lots of hilarity!

Never mind, while trying to wash lumps of custard out of your hair with a bucket of cold seawater, you can dream up even worse things to do to your victims when it's your turn to be King Neptune....

How can I go cruising if my parents don't?

If you don't have a relative or family friend to take you, there are various sailing organisations and charities that can get you cruising from as young as 12.

If you live in the UK, get hold of a brochure called 'Sail to Adventure' produced by ASTO

(Association of Sea Training Organisations - www.asto.org.uk). This is a list of sailing schools and charities which take young people to sea. You don't need any previous experience to sail with an ASTO organisation - they will take a landlubber and turn you into a sailor! Many offer RYA courses too.

Choose from a wide range of boats - from a modern yacht in the English Channel to a square rigged ship across the Atlantic!

Don't be discouraged if you're disabled in any way - many organisations (particularly RYA Sailability and the Jubilee Trust) cater for mixed abilities. The Jubilee Trust even has two big barques (Lord Nelson and Tenacious) designed to include wheelchair users.

Outside the UK, Sail Training International (www.sailtraininginternational.org) can tell you what organisations in other countries can help youngsters get to sea.

The STI also organises the Tall Ships' Race which takes place every year.

We were just off Tahiti when the next storm struck....

So do you have to be rich to go cruising?

No. Cruising can cost nothing at all if you learn the *skills* and offer to crew for other people – there are many *skippers* out there who have a *boat* and need help to *sail* her. If you get really good, one day you can get paid for sailing.

When the time comes to buy your own boat, it can be as cheap or expensive as you like; you don't need a millionaire's yacht to go sailing any more than you need a top of the range car to go driving. If you're prepared to start off with a small secondhand boat, start saving. That's what Ellen MacArthur did!

If you want to sail with an ASTO organisation but genuinely can't afford it, there may be grants or bursaries that could help you. ASTO can also give advice on how to raise funds. Sailing is a challenge available to everyone, whatever their circumstances!

Fancy sailing a brig like this? The Tall Ships Youth Trust has two of them, Prince William and Stavros S Niarchos. For more information about all these organisations, look in 'Useful websites and addresses' at the back of this book.

The Ocean Youth Club is one of several organisations that can teach you to sail a modern ketch like this....

What is a Turk's head and how do you make one?

A Turk's head is a decorative knot, not too difficult to learn and useful in lots of ways. You often see one round the tiller, or round the wheel to show the helm amidships position. You can make one into a bracelet, or flatten it out into a carrick mat. Get good at it and your boat could end up covered in Turk's heads!

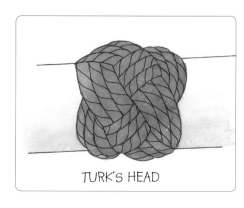

TURK'S HEAD

How do you make one?

You'll need plenty of rope - not too fat and not too thin. Have a look in the chandlery when you go ashore as there are many different colours and types to choose from. Rope is measured by diameter - 3 metres of 6mm braided line would be a good size for small hands to practise with. Follow the steps carefully and have a go; you'll soon get the hang of it.

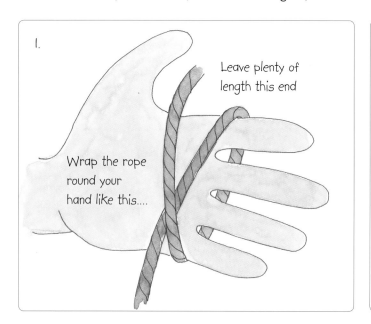

1.

Leave plenty of length this end

Wrap the rope round your hand like this....

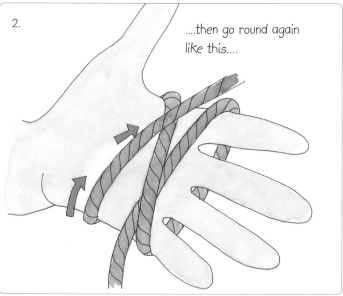

2.

....then go round again like this....

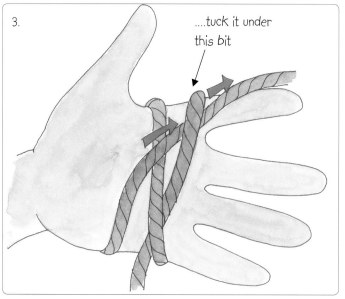

3.

....tuck it under this bit

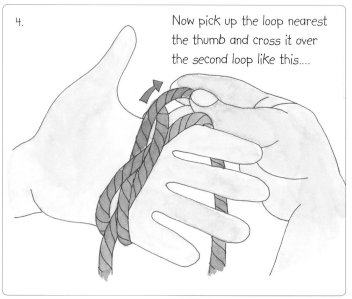

4.

Now pick up the loop nearest the thumb and cross it over the second loop like this....

5.
Check that your hand looks like this....

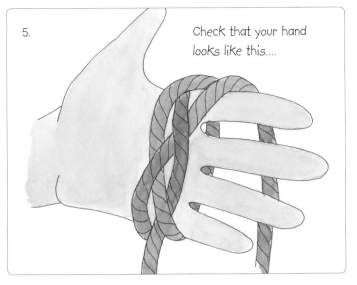

6.
Now look at the top of your hand. Take your free end over then under like this....

under over

7.
Next, turn your hand over. The back should look like this....

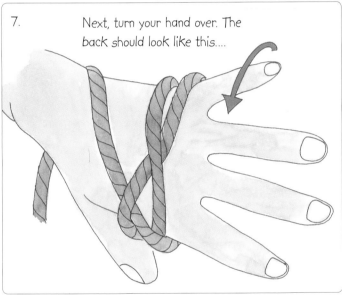

8.
Take the free end over then under again....

over under

9.
Pull one loop over the other, like you did at the front....

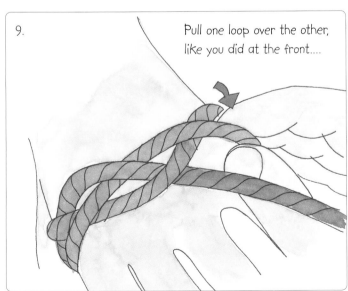

10.
under

....then take the free end over and under again.

over

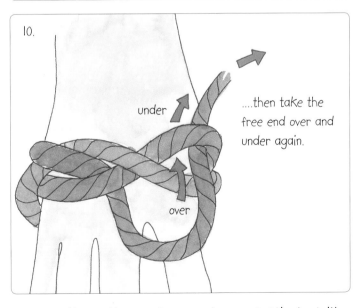

You're nearly there – can you begin to see the pattern of alternating unders and overs? It's just like a plait, only made with one strand not three.

If you get in a muddle, start again and take it slowly....

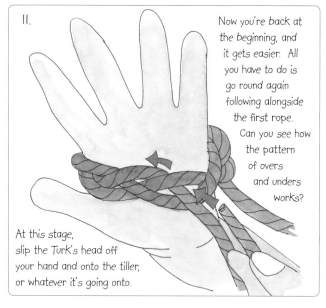

11.

Now you're back at the beginning, and it gets easier. All you have to do is go round again following alongside the first rope. Can you see how the pattern of overs and unders works?

At this stage, slip the Turk's head off your hand and onto the tiller, or whatever it's going onto.

Turk's heads can be made bigger or smaller than this, depending on what size rope you use and how wide the object is that you wrap it around. The one shown here has five main loops in it - flatten it out to see the pattern - but you can do more if you want to. Using a smaller rope (say 4mm) round your hand will probably give you seven loops round.

A loop in nautical language is called a 'bight' and each time round is called a 'lead', so if you want to impress your skipper you can call this is a 'three lead, five bight Turk's head'!

If you want to turn your Turk's head into a bracelet, you can varnish it so that it holds its shape.

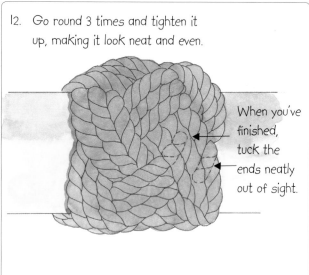

12. Go round 3 times and tighten it up, making it look neat and even.

When you've finished, tuck the ends neatly out of sight.

How do you turn a Turk's head into a carrick mat?

A carrick mat is a flattened out Turk's head. Start off a Turk's head in the usual way, then slip it off your hand and lay it flat. Carry on following the pattern round as many times as you can.

Make sure the beginning and the end of the rope are in the same place and tucked out of sight. Try to make sure each bight is the same size so the mat is a nice even shape.

13.

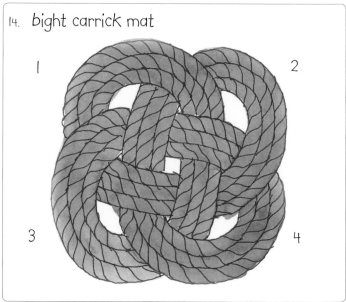

14. bight carrick mat

1   2

3   4

'Joshua' and the Porpoises

There are many mysterious tales about the sea - here is just one of them....

Frenchman Bernard Moitessier spent many years sailing his steel Ketch 'Joshua' round the world, much of it single handed. Once, close to New Zealand, he saw a school of porpoises acting strangely. They swam alongside him and then Kept veering off to the right, beating their tails on the water and making a noise to attract his attention.

After this had happened several times the puzzled sailor turned his ship to the right too. One porpoise then leapt clear of the water and somersaulted twice, after which all the porpoises returned to normal, following the boat for several hours before swimming away.

Checking his position, Moitessier found to his amazement that he had been sailing off course. If he hadn't turned to starboard when he did, 'Joshua' would have been wrecked on a reef!

Sailing Superstitions

Sailors have always been superstitious - some still are! It was bad luck to launch a boat on a Friday, bad luck to sail on a Friday, and very bad luck to have a woman on board! So if you're a woman sailor who likes to head off to sea after work on Friday evening, these superstitions will have to be thrown overboard.... but it's still bad luck to whistle on board as it is said to bring strong winds (unless it's flat calm and a wind is just what you need!).

Albatross are impressive big seabirds who live far from land in the wild Southern Ocean. Each albatross was said to be the soul of a drowned sailor so they used to be treated with respect and it was very unlucky indeed to Kill one. But these birds are now under serious threat of extinction, and many famous sailors are giving their support to a campaign to help them. See Useful websites page to find out more.

SAILING ROUND THE WORLD - More than two thirds of the planet is ocean - made for sailors, except for some *big* lumps of land in the way! Look at a globe. Turn it with the Pacific Ocean towards you to get an idea of just how much water there is out there.

Let's look at a map of the world from a sailor's point of view. With the right boat - not necessarily a big one - and enough time, all the oceans of the world are yours....

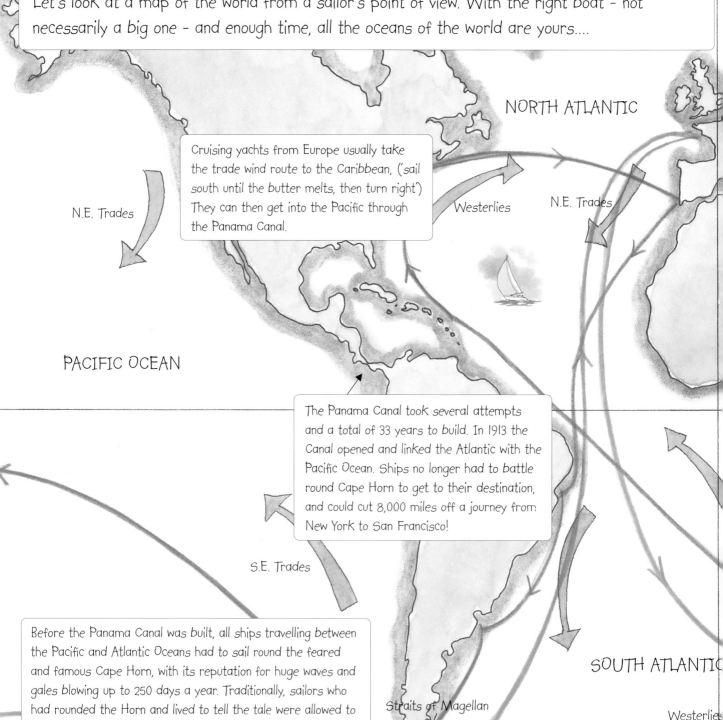

NORTH ATLANTIC

Cruising yachts from Europe usually take the trade wind route to the Caribbean, ('sail south until the butter melts, then turn right') They can then get into the Pacific through the Panama Canal.

N.E. Trades

Westerlies

N.E. Trades

PACIFIC OCEAN

The Panama Canal took several attempts and a total of 33 years to build. In 1913 the Canal opened and linked the Atlantic with the Pacific Ocean. Ships no longer had to battle round Cape Horn to get to their destination, and could cut 8,000 miles off a journey from New York to San Francisco!

S.E. Trades

Before the Panama Canal was built, all ships travelling between the Pacific and Atlantic Oceans had to sail round the feared and famous Cape Horn, with its reputation for huge waves and gales blowing up to 250 days a year. Traditionally, sailors who had rounded the Horn and lived to tell the tale were allowed to wear an earring in their left ear!

SOUTH ATLANTIC

Westerlies

Straits of Magellan

Cape Horn

Westerlies

ANTARTICA

Who sailed round the world alone first?

In 1895 American Joshua Slocum set off from Boston to sail round the world in his home built 37 foot Ketch 'Spray'. He had less than $2 in cash, but raised money on the way round by charging people a fee to look round his boat as well as giving lectures about his voyage. He arrived safely home after three years and two months!

This was in the days before yachts had engines, self steering gear or accurate navigation!

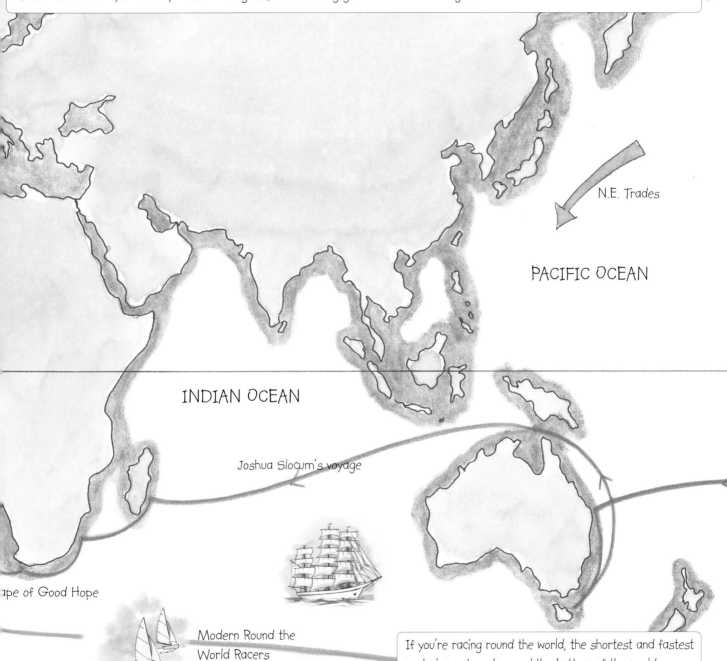

N.E. Trades

PACIFIC OCEAN

INDIAN OCEAN

Joshua Slocum's voyage

ape of Good Hope

Modern Round the World Racers

Westerlies

SOUTHERN OCEAN

If you're racing round the world, the shortest and fastest route is westwards round the bottom of the world, catching the strong winds at 40 degrees south (the Roaring Forties) or even 50 degrees (the Furious Fifties).

The Southern Ocean is a wild and dangerous place - westerly winds blow round the globe unhindered by land. Gales, icebergs and mountainous seas are normal down here!

What makes a good crew?

Know what everything on the boat is called and what it does

Enter the boat's position in the log book regularly

Keep everything stowed and tidy below decks

Get up on time when it's your turn on watch

Coil ropes neatly and tie knots that work

Look after your own safety – never need
reminding to use lifejacket and harness

Do something as soon as it's needed

Learn how to avoid collisions

Help to hoist and trim sails

Steer a straight course

Be a good lookout

Have fun!

YOU MUST THEN KNOW THE SEA....AND NOT
FORGET IT WAS MEANT TO BE SAILED OVER

JOSHUA SLOCUM

If you've done a bit of cruising and read this book, you'll have learnt a lot of boaty words. Here are some reminders in case you forget what they all mean....

Aft	towards the back of the boat
Anchor	holds the boat in place because it's heavy and dug into the sea bed!
Anticyclone	weather system bringing settled conditions
Astern	behind you!
Autopilot	electronic steering device
Backing	wind changing direction anti-clockwise, eg. changing from southerly to easterly
Backstay	wire that helps hold the mast up at the back of the boat
Barometer	measures air pressure and helps forecast the weather
Beam	the width of the boat at its widest part
Beam reach	sailing with the wind on the side of the boat
Bear away	turn the boat downwind
Bearing	using the degrees on a compass to measure direction
Beat	sailing upwind by zig-zagging either side of the no go zone
Beaufort	Admiral Beaufort devised the Beaufort Scale to measure wind strength
Boom	the foot of the sail is attached to this
Bow	pointy end!
Bow roller	fitting on the bow to take the anchor chain or mooring rope
Bow thruster	propeller at the front of the boat used for slow speed manoeuvring
Bowline	useful knot when you need a fixed loop (not to be confused with bow line which is a mooring line coming from the bow)
Buoyancy aid	helps a swimmer to stay afloat
Burgee	small hoisted flag to show your sailing club
Cam cleat	similar to 'jammer'
Chart	map for sailors
Chart datum	depth of water shown on chart – (also known as Lowest Astronomical Tide or LAT). Chart datum is the minimum amount of water shown – there will usually be more depending on state of tide.

ANCHOR

BOWLINE

Chart plotter	Electronic chart and gps which shows your position on a screen
Cleat	metal or wood fitting to attach ropes to (and stub your toes on if you're not careful!)

CLEAT

Clew	outside corner of a sail
Close hauled	sailing as close to the wind as you can go
Close reach	halfway between a beam reach and close hauled
Clove hitch	useful knot for tying a rope to a post
Companionway	entrance to a cabin, usually down steps or a ladder
Compass rose	compass printed onto a chart to help you navigate
Control line	attached to a furling jib to pull it in and let it out
Cruising chute	big lightweight downwind sail
Danbuoy	highly visible float thrown to a man overboard
Depression	weather system bringing rain and wind
Draught	depth of a boat below the water line

Ease	let out a rope gently and under control (eg. ease sheet)
Ebb	tide going out

DRAUGHT

Echo sounder	electronic device which measures depth of water
Ensign	flag showing a boat's nationality
Fairlead	metal fitting to help a rope lead smoothly from boat to shore

FAIRLEAD

Fender	squidgy plastic cushion which protects the side of the boat in harbour
Fiddle rail	rim around worktops and tables in a cabin to stop things sliding on
Flares	like fireworks – set these off in an emergency so you can be seen by rescuers
Flood (tide)	tide coming in
Flybridge	open air steering position at the top of a motor cruiser
Foot	bottom edge of a sail
Fore	towards the front of the boat
Forecabin (foc'sle)	small cabin at the front

Foredeck	deck space at front of the boat
Forestay	wire holding the mast up at the front. Jib is attached to this.
Furling	system of rolling up a sail – usually a jib
Galley	boat kitchen
Gimbals	allow an object like a cooker (or a compass) to stay level even when the boat is moving
GPS	(global positioning system) clever electronic device that uses satellites to locate your exact position
Greenwich meridian	zero degrees of longitude. Go to the Greenwich Observatory in London if you want to stand on it!
Guardrail	wires or rails round the boat to help stop you falling overboard
Gybe	bring the wind around the stern of the boat so that the sails change sides
Gybe oh	What the helmsman shouts to warn the crew as the boom starts to come across
Halyard	(sometimes spelt 'halliard') rope that pulls up or lowers down a sail
Hanks	clips that attach a sail to a stay (eg. a jib to a forestay)
Harness	worn to clip your lifeline to so you stay attached to the boat if you fall overboard (some lifejackets have lifeline attachments)
Head	boat word for the toilet
Head up	steer the boat closer towards the wind
Heel	a sailing boat heels over with the pressure of wind in her sails
Helm	the wheel or tiller that steers a boat; also the person doing the steering
Isobars	lines of equal pressure on a weather chart
Jackstay	line running along the deck of a boat to attach your lifeline to
Jammer	locking device for ropes which enables quick release. Keep your fingers clear when using these!
Jib	small sail at the front of the boat, set from the forestay
Jib sheets	control the jib
Keel	heavy weight at the bottom of a sailing yacht to counterbalance the pressure of wind in the sails and help her go forwards instead of sideways!
Kicker	control line between base of the mast and the boom to hold the boom down

Kill cord	emergency device attached to an outboard which stops the engine if you fall overboard
Latitude	Imaginary lines going parallel round the globe east to west (the biggest one is the equator)
Lee cloth	made of strong canvas or netting, it holds you into your bunk if the boat is heeled over
Lee oh	what the helmsman calls out when tacking as the boat comes through the wind
Lee shore	when the wind is blowing off the sea and onto the land – dangerous for sailing boats in strong winds!
Leech	back edge of a sail
Leeward	the downwind side
Lifebuoy	thrown over the side to help a man overboard stay afloat
Lifejacket	keeps a non swimmer fully afloat with their head clear of the water
Lifeline	connects you to the boat (as long as it's attached at both ends!)
Liferaft	emergency inflatable craft that helps keep you safe if your boat sinks
Log book	where the navigator keeps track of where you are and where you're going
Longitude	imaginary lines running round the globe north to south
Low water	low tide
Luff	the luff of a sail is the forward edge. To luff the boat means head into wind and make the luff of the sail flap
Magnetic	a compass points to the magnetic north pole – which is not in the same place as the physical north pole
Mainsail	big sail attached to the mast and boom
Mainsheet	controls the mainsail
Make fast	secure a piece of rope so it doesn't slip
Navigation buoy	warns you of dangers or tells you where safe water is, according to its shape and colour
Neap tide	not as high and not as low as a spring tide
Outdrive	when the engine is inside the boat and the gearbox and propeller are outside
Painter	mooring line attached to a dinghy
Planing	skimming over the water very fast
Port	left hand side of the boat (goes with the colour red)
Preventer	line attached to the boom to stop an accidental gybe

Pulpit	metal rail at the bow of the boat
Pushpit	metal rail at the stern of the boat
Quarter	between the stern and the beam – port quarter and starboard quarter
Radar	allows you to see large objects, such as other boats and the shore
Raft up	lots of boats all tied up together
Reef	make the sail smaller in a strong wind
Round turn and two half hitches	another useful knot for securing a rope to a post or rail (also good for tying fenders)
Rowlock	your oars rest in these when you're rowing the dinghy
Rudder	connected to the tiller, determines the direction of the boat
Run	sailing with the wind directly behind you
Running rigging	all the ropes on a sailing boat that move (eg. because they control the sails)
Shackle	attaches a rope to a sail
Sheet bend	useful knot for attaching two pieces of rope together
Shrouds	wires holding up the mast at the sides of the boat
Skipper	the boss!
Soundings	depth of water (either shown on the chart, or readings from your echo sounder)
Spinnaker	big balloon shaped downwind sail
Spring tide	biggest tidal range because the sun and moon are lined up
Stanchion	posts around the edge of the boat with guardrails attached
Standing rigging	fixed wires and ropes that support the mast
Starboard	right hand side (colour green)
Stern	back end of the boat
Synoptic chart	weather map
Tack	bottom front corner of a sail. Also to change direction by bringing the wind around the front of the boat
Take a turn	loop a rope around a cleat to help take the strain
Telltale	string or ribbons attached to sails to show if the sails are properly trimmed

ROWLOCKS

SHACKLES

Tidal stream	how fast the tide is flowing
Tiller	stick attached to the rudder – move this to steer the boat
Toe rail	edge of the deck – bit you stand on when climbing aboard
Topping lift	holds the boom up when the sail is down
Trim	trimming sails means setting them in the right position for the wind direction
Trim tab	metal flaps which force the back of the boat up or down
True	true north is the physical north pole (a bit different to the magnetic pole)
Twin screw	double engine on a motor cruiser
Veering	change in wind direction in a clockwise direction (eg. north to east)
Vhf/dsc radio	two way radio used for communicating with other ships and also calling for help in an emergency
Warp	another word for a mooring line
Waypoint	position programmed into a gps as steps along a journey
Winch	helps to wind in a sheet or halyard when it gets too hard to pull by hand
Windlass	lifts anchors
Windward	side the wind is blowing from

There will be more sea words to learn as you go, but the more cruising you do, the easier it will get - even on a square rigger!

No no no.... I said the fore lower t'gallant sheet not the main upper topsail downhaul!!

Royal Yachting Association   www.rya.org.uk

RYA House, Ensign Way

Hamble, Southampton,

Hampshire, SO31 4YA

Trusts and Charities that take unaccompanied youngsters sailing:

Association of Sea Training Organisations

Unit 10, North Meadow

Royal Clarence Yard

Gosport

Hampshire PO12 1BP   www.asto.org.uk

ASTO is the UK's umbrella organisation for youth offshore sailing schemes, ranging from tall ships to small ships; ASTO can also advise about grants and fundraising activities.

For more about tall ships activities in the UK and world wide:

Sail Training International

5 Mumby Road

Gosport

Hampshire PO12 1AA   www.sailtraininginternational.org

STI is a registered charity with worldwide membership. Its purpose is the development and education of young people of all nationalities, cultures, religions and social backgrounds through the sail training experience.

Sailing with Disabilities:

RYA Sailability   www.rya.org.uk

Jubilee Trust   www.jst.org.uk

International Association for Disabled Sailing   www.sailing.org/disabled

For information on the environment and wildlife at sea:

For environmental information and advice: www.thegreenblue.org.uk

Report sightings of whales and dolphins to Whale and Dolphin Conservation Society:

www.wdcs.org.uk

Information about sea birds from the RSPB   www.rspb.org.uk

More about the endangered albatross   www.savethealbatross.net

Information about protection of wildlife at sea from the Marine Wildlife Conservation Society
www.mcsuk.org.uk

Safety At Sea:

RNLI (Royal National Lifeboat Institution)   www.rnli.co.uk
Support the RNLI by becoming a member; children's membership called Stormforce is also available.

The RNLI have a special sea safety website   www.rnli.org.uk/seasafety

They also have an education website with children's activities at:
www.rnli-shorething.org.uk

MCA (Maritime and Coastguard Agency)   www.mcga.gov.uk
Responsible for safety at sea and around the coast, the coastguard co-ordinates search and rescue operations.

The RNLI and MCA produce a useful series of safety leaflets called Sea Safety Guidelines.

More background on the history of sailing and navigation:

National Maritime Museum, Greenwich, and the Royal Observatory

www.nmm.ac.uk

Maritime Museum Falmouth   www.nmmc.co.uk

Bibliography

RYA Publications (available from www.rya.org.uk)

RYA Competent Crew Handbook

RYA Day Skipper Handbook

RYA Weather Handbook

RYA Motor Cruising Handbook

RYA Flag Etiquette and Visual Signals

International Regulations for Prevention of Collisions at Sea

Other publications used to help write this book:

Log Book for Children by Claudia Myatt (Starfish Books)

'A Voyage for Madmen' by Peter Nichols (Profile Books)

'Sailing Alone Round the World' by Joshua Slocum

'Handbook of Knots' by Des Pawson (Dorling Kindersley)

'SMART SAILOR' AWARD

Name: . . . .

This is to certify that the above named has impressed the skipper by being a helpful, safe and seaworthy crew member of the good ship:

. . . .

(name of vessel)

Signed: . . . . (Skipper)   Date: . . . .

'SMART SAILOR' AWARD

Name: . . . .

This is to certify that the above named has impressed the skipper by being a helpful, safe and seaworthy crew member of the good ship:

. . . .

(name of vessel)

Signed: . . . . (Skipper)   Date: . . . .

RYA Go Cruising!

Words and Illustrations by: Claudia Myatt
Edited by: Simon Jinks, RYA Chief Cruising Instructor

© RYA 2006
First Published 2006

The Royal Yachting Association
RYA House
Ensign Way
Hamble
Southampton
SO31 4YA

Tel: 0845 345 0400
Fax: 0845 345 0329
E-mail: publications@rya.org.uk
Web: www.rya.org.uk

ISBN: 1905104332
RYA Order Code: G42

Totally Chlorine Free   Sustainable Forests

Cover Design: Claudia Myatt
Typeset: Creativebyte
Proofreading and indexing: Alan Thatcher
Printed in: China through World Print